Careers in
Health and Fitness

Careers in
Health and Fitness

by
Jackie Heron, RN

THE ROSEN PUBLISHING GROUP, INC
New York

Published in 1990 by The Rosen Publishing Group, Inc.
29 East 21st Street, New York, NY 10010

Copyright 1988, 1990 by Jackie Heron, RN

Revised Edition 1990

Library of Congress Cataloging-in-Publication Data

Heron, Jackie.
  Careers in health and fitness / by Jackie Heron. — 1st ed.
166p. cm. — (Careers in depth)
  Includes index.
  ISBN 0-8239-1162-4
  1. Physical fitness—Vocational guidance—United States.
2. Health—Vocational guidance—United States. I. Title
II. Series.
GV510.U5H47 1988   87-35659
613.7'023'73—dc19   CIP

Manufactured in the United States of America

Acknowledgments

I would like to thank Ruth Rosen, my editor, for her guidance, patience, and encouragement as I wrote this book.

A big thank-you to the health and fitness professionals I photographed and interviewed. Each of your contributions added new dimensions to the concepts presented herein.

A special thank-you to my husband, Ross Heron, for the photographs he contributed and for his loving support.

The acknowledgments would not be complete without thanks to Renee Dunham, my word processor, for an excellent job. Special thanks also to Chuck Ternes for his superb photographs.

My thanks to the Franklin Racquet Club and the Kenlock Clinic for the photograph opportunities.

Introduction

This book is designed to acquaint you with the diverse opportunities and responsibilities of a career in health and fitness. The information presented is intellectually stimulating, current, and factual, yet interesting. Each chapter contains supplemental guides which, when used with the text, will enhance your personal awareness and assist you in evaluating your probability of success in the field of health and fitness.

The supplemental guides will be indispensable assets if you follow these suggestions:

- Keep in mind there are no right or wrong answers, only your opinion of what is best for you.
- You should respond to each question as completely and accurately as possible, to gain maximum insight into your probability of success in a given career.
- Guard against interjecting someone else's expectations of you. Try to identify your true feelings, not what you think your best friend thinks they should be, lest you defeat your own efforts.
- A comprehensive and meticulous review of your answers will reveal interesting facts about yourself, and might educe a particular expertise previously unknown to you.
- Remember, your responses are subject to change as you accumulate the self-knowledge necessary to infer vital

career decisions. Hence, it may behoove you to periodically evaluate and, if appropriate, revise your answers.

The use of the pronouns *he* and *she* has been avoided. Although gender plays a significant role in your career choice, your gender should be the implicit, not the dominant, factor. Examine your personal attributes, attitudes, philosophies, personal preferences, desires, and expectations to determine your career choice. Remember, everything that makes you uniquely you is gender-influenced.

Contents

Chapter I

You Have Just Entered The Health and Fitness Zone

The parameters of the health and fitness zone defy traditional boundaries. Look around you, anywhere. You will see health-conscious people striving to meet their personal fitness goals.

As you sit idly staring out your living-room window, you see a runner in motion. If you focus your attention on the athlete long enough, an aura of dedication and intensity envelops you. This "runner interference" has induced you to evaluate your own health and fitness status, perhaps updating your priorities.

Lingering in the mall, you check your watch and realize that you are going to be late for class if you do not hurry. Knowing you will miss dinner, you buy a bag of potato chips and a candy bar as a substitute. En route to your car, you are encircled by a group of patrons leaving the sporting goods and health food stores. Stopping to allow the crowd to disperse, you take inventory of their purchases: tennis rackets, weightlifting equipment, a bag of health foods, golf clubs, baseball glove, another bag of health foods, and health club apparel. Your thoughts quickly shift to the class you must attend. You hurry to your car, choking down your potato chips and candy bar. On the way you pass several of

"Runner interference" envelops you.

the shoppers, who by now have separated into small groups of friends. Their happiness seems to mesmerize you as they discuss their favorite fitness activity and savor morsels of health food. Once in your car and driving to class, that excitement is behind you. Or is it? Conscious efforts to concentrate are thwarted by haunting images and echoes of the health and fitness enthusiasts you encountered at the mall.

You and a friend are viewing a television documentary on the many varieties of workout programs. During the commercials, you discuss the content of the program, but one advertisement draws your attention back to the screen. A male and a female are featured, both in excellent physical condition, and the announcer proclaims, "You can look like this . . . IF you join OUR health spa!" The announcer then details the virtues of the spa's workout. The key points highlighted in the commercial match the closing commentary on the health and fitness documentary. Do you read the message? The virtues of a fitness workout are not restricted to one type.

You arrive a few minutes early for a doctor's appointment. To pass the time, you flip through a health and fitness magazine and pause at an ad for a weight-loss clinic: "Lose weight and keep it off!" Adding credibility to the clinic's claims, a fellow patient volunteers a convincing testimonial of having lost 35 pounds through a supportive weight-loss clinic. This person's self-discipline, commitment, and success convey a winning style you cannot forget.

The parameters of the health and fitness zone are all around you. People of all ages, from all walks of life, engage in an infinite number of health and fitness activities. Think for a minute and then answer these questions.

- How many people do you know who routinely participate in physical activity?
- What physical activities do they pursue?
- Do they exercise alone, such as using a stationary bike at home, or are they members of an organized team, such as baseball?
- Is their activity structured, as in an aerobics class, or is it flexible, as with two friends in a tennis rally?

What did your responses tell you? Society's growing awareness of the need to be fit and healthy has created a wealth of employment possibilities for qualified personnel. Careers in the health and fitness industry are expanding at a rate that presages continued growth during the next decade to accommodate the technological advances and the everchanging needs of our culture. This is an excellent time to capitalize on society's needs, while simultaneously structuring an exciting career.

You must be able to answer career-related questions like these before you can choose the best career for you.

- Do you have a personal commitment to health and fitness for yourself and others?
- Have you established your career aspirations? Are your goals appropriate for your choice?
- Do you have the motivation to excel?
- Is your personality type compatible with your career choice?
- Are you dedicated and willing to undertake the educational preparation necessary to succeed?

With these questions in mind, preview the following categories of careers and try to name a few specific careers that might fit into each category.

CATEGORIES OF HEALTH AND FITNESS CAREERS

The careers explored in this book represent a cross section of the universally recognized health and fitness careers. Each category describes careers that share basic components: similar primary functions, fundamental skills, educational preparation, and personality types.

Category A introduces several career options as a *Health and Fitness Adviser*. Professional health and fitness advisers perform services to enhance a client's athletic proficiency. These services include evaluating the client's basic abilities and offering supportive, instructional counseling intended to perfect the client's expertise and provide therapeutic treatment of physiological dysfunctions.

Category B covers career opportunities for *Health and Fitness Instructors*. "Instructor" is an ambiguous term for persons whose primary function is to prepare and conduct health and fitness programs. These programs address the diversified demands of all age groups and skill levels: infants to grandparents, leisure learners to professional athletes. An innovative mind could create its own empire in this field.

Category C, Destination Chief Executive Officer (CEO), covers managerial roles available in the health and fitness zone.

Category D, Media Talk, accents health and fitness careers in communication. The communications expert must be adept at delivering a powerful message. Do you capture your friends' attention with your photography, your written accounts of sporting events, or your ability to generate excitement with your manner of speech?

Category E, Health and Fitness Retail Sales, encompasses a broad spectrum of careers in sales, from employee to chief executive officer.

Your career exploration can be sophisticated or simple, structured or flexible, as long as it meets your needs. Remember, you are planning your tomorrows with your ideas of today.

Chapter II presents the Career Exploration Fact Sheets necessary to begin your project. With these fact sheets you will identify career facts applicable to your situation and examine your personal characteristics that will influence your career choice.

Chapter III deals with your educational preparation. You will become acquainted with the different forms of educational program you may pursue, find the teaching institutions that offer the program you are seeking, and follow the required admission procedures.

Next you will calculate your expected monetary expenditures and your available resources and prepare your financial statement.

Chapter IV continues your career exploration through the various aspects of identifying job-finding sources, preparing your job-winning package, and using it to obtain the position you want.

Chapter II

Career Choices in Health and Fitness

As you read Chapter II you will become acquainted with a wide assortment of career choices in the health and fitness zone, organized into a series of Career Exploration Fact Sheets. You read the Fact Sheet and mentally analyze the career facts as they pertain to you. Then you write your analysis of that career on a Career Exploration Rating Sheet, which allows you to rate its advantages and deficiencies according to your personal standards.

A typical Career Exploration Fact Sheet provides the following information:

Primary Functions: Reveals the duties you are expected to perform.

Fundamental Skills: Suggests the most common learned and natural skills displayed by successful persons. If your outstanding skills are not listed, ask yourself if your skills would help you effectively carry out the primary function. If you say yes, add your skills to the list. Perhaps the most valuable fundamental skill you can strive for is the ability to integrate your technical expertise, people/social skills, and general talents into a refined series of actions, reactions, and interactions that will foster professional competence.

Advantageous Features: Outlines a few of the desirable characteristics of the career.

Questionable Features: Highlights characteristics you may or may not like. You are the judge.

Basic Equipment: Mentions equipment used in each career when appropriate.

Employment Possibilities: Examines the organizations, companies, or businesses that employ these professionals.

Formal Education and Specialty Training: Suggests an acceptable level of preparation for entry-level employment in the career. However, the requirements can vary from state to state. To procure specific information, write to the governing association identified under the heading *Universities or Associations* on the Fact Sheet, or to the certification or licensing board (see next heading).

Certification and Licensing Regulations: Noted only when applicable. Health and fitness advisers are usually licensed and board-certified. Check these regulations carefully. To qualify to take the state boards, you must graduate from an accredited educational program, file an application for licensure, and pay the fee. State boards are given several times a year and are administered, proctored, and controlled by the individual board. Licensure or certification is mandated by state or federal law.

Universities or Associations: Lists one or more universities or associations that specialize in this career.

Salary Range: Salaries quoted are estimated averages. Exact salary is determined by a multitude of variables. Consider the impact of these factors on your salary range.

- Are your credentials (certified, licensed, formal education, specialty training) superior to those of your competitor? Your degree of expertise can affect your pay. Some employers pay a premium for years of experience, and most give financial rewards according to your degree or continuing education.

- Does the demand for your services exceed the supply of qualified professionals available? Irregular shifts such as second and third receive a percentage more per hour than their day counterparts, and a premium is sometimes paid for holidays, overtime, and weekends.
- Geographical location also influences salaries. The East Coast generally pays more than the South, and the Midwest more than the West. If you work in a rural setting, chances are good that you will receive less than your equal in a metropolitan area.

Advancement Is Attained: Explains general accomplishments that can lead to advancement.

CATEGORY A—HEALTH AND FITNESS ADVISERS

Part I—Physicians
- Sports Physician
  M.D. (Doctor of Medicine); D.O. (Doctor of Osteopathy)
- Sports Orthopedic Surgeon
- Sports Podiatrist D.P.M. (Doctor of Podiatric Medicine)
- Sports Chiropractor
- —Sports Physician's Assistant

Part II—Research Specialists
- Educational Biomechanics Research Scientist
- Educational Exercise Physiologist
- Medical Biomechanics Research Scientist
- Medical Exercise Physiologist
- Sports Sociologist

Part III—Think and Eat Healthy
- Sports Nutritionist
- —Sports Nutrition Counselor
- Sports Psychologist

Part IV—Muscle Movement
- Exercise Testing Technician
- Physical Therapist
- —Physical Therapist Assistant

Health and Fitness Advisers provide an indispensable service to the health and fitness enthusiasts of our society. Each profession contributes its own unique expertise; however, the principal objective of a health and fitness adviser is to help clients achieve peak performance with a minimum of effort and as free of pain as possible.

These professions offer numerous benefits: an abundance of employment opportunities, job security, stability, and longevity, plus a lucrative salary.

Health and fitness advisers generally can expect these entry-level prerequisites:

- Maintain a grade point average (GPA) of 3.5 or higher, with a curriculum emphasis on mathematics and science.
- Display the ability to master a carefully structured educational program with concise learning objectives.
- Take and pass the national or state boards of the state in which you will practice before being licensed. In some instances, board certification is also required.

Part I—Physicians

Sports medicine professionals strive to promote health by curing or stabilizing illnesses or injuries and augmenting or perfecting the client's athletic performance by developing a training program designed to meet each client's needs.

Sports Physicians—Career Exploration Fact Sheet

Career Choice: M.D. (Doctor of Medicine); D.O. (Doctor of Osteopathy)
- The major distinction between an M.D. and a D.O. is that the D.O. incorporates musculoskeletal manipulation into the treatment plan, whereas the M.D. relies on other forms of medical intervention (surgery and medication).

Primary Functions:
- Evaluate a client's ability (physical, emotional, psychological) to meet the minimum standards of the activity the client wishes to undertake. This is usually done by taking a medical history and making a physical examination.
- Diagnose and treat ailments interfering with a client's performance.
- Monitor an injured or ill client's rehabilitation progress, and approve the date the client may safely return to action.
- Inform support personnel (coach or trainer) of individualized training planned for each client.
- Measure and fit each client with protective gear appropriate to the activity.

Formal Education and Specialty Training: University premedical training and medical school, followed by clinical practicum as an intern and resident. Specialty training is required in the sport you plan to serve.

Universities or Associations:

Association of American
  Medical Colleges
One DuPont Circle NW
  Washington, DC 20036

American Osteopathic
  Association
212 East Ohio Street
  Chicago, IL 60611

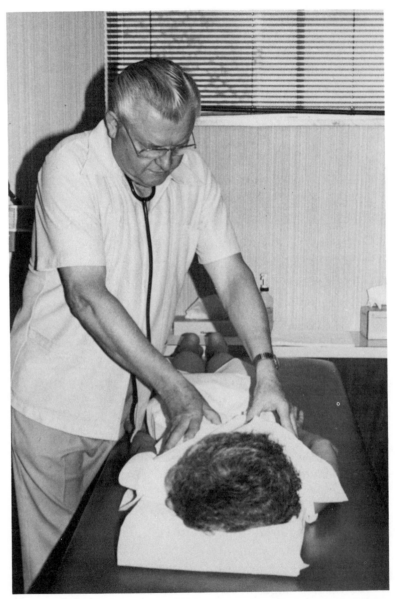

An osteopath prepares to do a back manipulation on a fitness client.

American Medical
Association
535 North Dearborn Street
Chicago, IL 60620
Salary Range: $50,000.

American College of Sports
Medicine
1440 Monroe Street
Madison, WI 53706

Career Choice: Sports Orthopedic Surgeon

Primary Functions:
- Diagnose and treat injuries or diseases affecting the musculoskeletal system (bones and muscles).
- Perform surgery to repair damaged muscles or bones.
- Instruct client in how to prevent future injuries.

Formal Education and Specialty Training: A degree as a sports physician, with a specialty in orthopedic surgery and a major in sports medicine.

Universities or Associations:
American Orthopedic Society for
Sports Medicine
60 West Hubbard Street
Chicago, IL 60610

Salary Range: $60,000 to $150,000 plus. Average can be $100,000 for a qualified orthopedic surgeon. Salary range variables include your competitors, your expertise, and your clientele.

Career Choice: Sports Podiatrist (D.P.M.)

Primary Functions:
- Diagnose and treat injuries and deformities of the legs and feet, especially the feet.
- Plan and implement personalized training programs for clients to prevent injuries.

Formal Education and Specialty Training: A degree as a doctor of podiatry, with specialty training in foot surgery, biomechanics, and sports medicine.

Universities or Associations:
American Academy of Podiatric
Sports Medicine
P.O. Box 31331
San Francisco, CA 94131

Salary Range: $50,000 plus.

Career Choice: Sports Chiropractor. This classification of physicians ordinarily does not prescribe medications or perform surgery.

Primary Functions:
- Evaluate and treat health and fitness-related injuries by manipulating the spinal cord to reestablish optimum musculoskeletal function and balance.
- Prescribe complementary therapy, including heat, ultrasound, or water treatment.
- Teach correct body mechanics to prevent future injuries.

Formal Education and Specialty Training: An associate degree (two years) in liberal arts followed by four years at an accredited chiropractic university. Specialty training requires a concentration in sports medicine.

Universities or Associations:
American Chiropractic Association
2220 Grand Avenue
Des Moines, IA 50312

Salary Range: $30,000 to $40,000. Financial recompense is slightly less than the others in this group, as are the educational requirements. A specialty in sports medicine increases the financial rewards.

Advantageous Features: Only a small number of chiropractors specialize in sports, substantially reducing the competition.

The information contained under the following headings is applicable to all the preceding physician career choices, unless otherwise stated.

Fundamental Skills:
- Ability to instruct, monitor, and supervise the non-medical and support personnel directing your clients' training program.
- Ability to extract specific knowledge from your client's medical background to facilitate accurate diagnosis and treatment.
- Ability to interpret and immediately apply new information is a skill worth perfecting.
- Manual dexterity is an asset.

Advantageous Features:
- Sports physicians are respected and appreciated by the general public.
- Your position is highly visible.
- You function in a superior working environment controlled almost exclusively by you.
- Your financial rewards are excellent.

Questionable Features:
- You must invest precious personal resources (time, energy, money) and be prepared to draw on your reserve as you enter the intensive and highly competitive educational/clinical preparation to become a sports physician.
- If relentless pressure to achieve in the classroom (theory) or in the field (clinical) intimidates you, now is the time to look elsewhere.

- Your work schedule may be unconventional. Irregular hours, overtime, and travel can be expected if you are responsible for a team, a club, or a private client who travels to meets.
- You might be asked to write work-related books or articles.
- You might be approached by the media to explain a fitness-related issue.

Basic Equipment: The conventional physician's kit (blood pressure cuff, pain medications, stethoscope, splints, wraps, bandages), and equipment designed for the activity you serve.

Employment Possibilities:
- You might establish a private practice.
- You might practice at a clinic, sharing your caseload with fellow sports physicians and support staff.
- Many hospitals have sports injury teams that include a sports physician.
- Medical schools affiliated with universities frequently have sports physicians on the staff.
- Some health and fitness-directed organizations employ sports physicians.
- Most organized sports, amateur or professional, welcome a qualified sports physician.
- Health and fitness-related private enterprises, including health clubs, resorts, and athletic clubs, employ sports physicians.

Certification and Licensing Regulations: You must take and pass a state and national board to be licensed to practice. Board certification is highly recommended or required. Consult your state licensing bureau and the representing association to verify requirements in your state.

Advancement Is Attained: By proven clinical and theoretical expertise. Universally recognized advancement is to Chief of Sports Medicine or Chief of Medical Staff.

Sports Physician's Assistant—Career Exploration Fact Sheet

This is a unique position for anyone interested in sports medicine, yet not interested in the extensive formal preparation necessary to become a sports physician.

Primary Functions:
- Act under the direction of a sports physician. The physician's assistant has greater responsibility than a registered nurse but less than the doctor.
- The assistant's role is governed by the physician in charge and by state and other regulatory agency rules.

Formal Education and Specialty Training: As might be expected, educational preparation is less than for a physician, but more than for a four-year registered nurse. Specialty training includes the area of expertise (e.g. orthopedic, podiatric) and a major in sports medicine.

Universities or Associations:

Association of American
  Medical Colleges
One DuPont Circle NW
Washington, DC 20036

American Osteopathic
  Association
212 East Ohio Street
Chicago, IL 60611

American Medical
  Association
535 North Dearborn Street
Chicago, IL 60620

American College of Sports
  Medicine
1440 Monroe Street
Madison, WI 53706

Salary Range: $30,000 to $50,000. Possibly higher depending on your credentials.

Certification and Licensing Regulations: Consult your state licensing bureau or association for details.

Advancement Is Attained: Through higher education and proven expertise.

References for Review

Helping Hands: Challenge of Medicine
   American Medical Association
   535 North Dearborn Street
   Chicago, IL 60610
Medicine—A Woman's Career
   American Medical Women's Association
   740 Broadway
   New York, NY 10019

Part II—Research Specialists

Research Specialists—Career Exploration Fact Sheet

Career Choice: Educational Biomechanics Research Scientist
Primary Functions:
 • Research the body mechanics of human musculo-skeletal movement.
 • Prepare technical papers for publication in connection with teaching at the university level.

Career Choice: Educational Exercise Physiologist

Primary Functions:
 • Research vital aspects of a client's performance, concentrating on cardiopulmonary capacity, endurance, strength, joint flexibility, muscle movement, and

the interrelated biological responses and resultant adaptations.

- Prepare technical papers for publication in connection with teaching at the university level.

Career Choice: Medical Biomechanics Research Scientist

Primary Functions:

- Research the complexities of a client's movements during physical activity.
- Correct abnormal musculoskeletal movement with appropriate equipment.
- These research studies yield blueprints for design of fitness equipment, which are valuable development tools for the manufacturers of such equipment.

Career Choice: Medical Exercise Physiologist

Primary Functions:

- Administer exercise tests to analyze a client's current level of performance (cardiopulmonary and musculo-skeletal status).
- Calculate the optimum level of performance.
- Evaluate the effectiveness of the client's present fitness training program, including any machines in use.
- Suggest program changes to achieve optimum performance.

Although not identical, these career choices bear a strong resemblance to one another in the remaining areas.

Fundamental Skills:

- Maintain concentration and strict attention to minute detail, unaffected by environmental and personal interruptions, sometimes for hours at a time.

- Be capable of planning, organizing, and conducting experiments from basic concept through conclusion.
- Gather, assemble, analyze, sort, classify, interpret, and translate pertinent data into layman's language.
- Teach on a college level.

Advantageous Features:
- This is your Utopia if you enjoy research, teaching, and writing.
- Although little known to the general public, you are an irreplaceable resource and authority to the health and fitness business and industry. The treatment plans of physicians and other professionals reflect the findings of your research papers. Manufacturers design their products according to your blueprints.

Questionable Features:
- You are compelled to meet deadlines, sometimes before expected, while handling massive amounts of technical data.
- If a fast pace intimidates you, or a lifetime of study turns you cold, now is the time to look elsewhere.

Employment Possibilities: Athletic programs (Special Olympics, professional teams, special-needs client programs), community organizations (YMCA and other clubs), private practice, rehabilitative programs, or a university campus.

Formal Education and Specialty Training: At least a master's, preferably a Ph.D. Specialty training is rigorous. Although there are slight differences in each field's requirements, the general studies recommended for undergraduate work for all four professions include human anatomy and physiology, the biological sciences, biomechanics, chemistry, computer science, environmental physiology, exercise biochemistry, exercise psychology, first aid, health education, kinesiology (human anatomy + body mechanics = human movement), laboratory techniques in exercise physiology, mathematics (including calculus), human motor skills (learning and development), nutrition, physical fitness evaluation, physics, psychology, research design, and statistics.

Certification and Licensing Regulations: To practice as an exercise physiologist or in biomechanics, you must be state-licensed and board-certified.

Universities or Associations:

American College of
   Sports Medicine
P.O. Box 1440
Indianapolis, IN 46206

Association for Research
   Administration
Professional Councils and
   Societies
1900 Association Drive
Reston, VA 22091

Salary Range: $25,000 to $35,000.

Advancement Is Attained: Through publication of comprehensive, academically sound research projects, and teaching aptitude. Biomechanics has excellent advancement potential in the large manufacturers area.

Sports Sociologist—Career Exploration Fact Sheet

Primary Functions:
- Understand the complexities of sports-related activities as a social process.
- Prepare technical papers for publication, in connection with teaching at the university level.

Fundamental Skills:
- Maintain concentration and strict attention to minute detail, unaffected by environmental and personal interruptions, sometimes for hours at a time.

- Gather, assemble, sort, classify, analyze, and translate pertinent data into layman's language.

Advantageous Features: Your time can be flexibly scheduled to meet teaching and research commitments.

Questionable Features:
- Several years of educational preparation are required.
- If social interaction bores you, now is the time to look elsewhere.

Employment Possibilities: Universities, medical centers, special-interest groups, clinics, and athletic programs.

Formal Education and Specialty Training: At least a master's, preferably a Ph.D. A master's in physical education with a *specialty* in sports sociology, or a master's in sociology with a concentration in physical education.

Certification and Licensing Regulations: State licensing and board certification are the rule.

Universities or Associations:
American College of Sports Medicine
P.O. Box 1440
Indianapolis, IN 46206

Salary Range: $25,000 to 35,000.

Advancement Is Attained: Through publication of technical research papers, and teaching expertise.

Part III—Think and Eat Healthy

Sports Nutritionist—Career Exploration Fact Sheet

Primary Functions:
- Analyze each client's dietetic needs.
- Plan a balanced diet that is realistic for each client to follow.

Fundamental Skills:
- Analyze your clients' total dietetic needs according to physical status and requirements imposed by their level of physical activity.
- Be realistic concerning clients' self-discipline to adhere to a specific regimen.

Advantageous Features:
- The projected need is increasing, and the supply of qualified nutritionists inadequate.
- As a nutritionist, you foster healthy eating habits and attitudes in your clients. The importance of good nutrition is frequently neglected in the health and fitness zone.

Questionable Features: Some clients can be unintentionally deceitful regarding their adherence to your prescribed diet. You must identify and counsel those clients whose noncompliance is jeopardizing their health or physical performance.

Employment Possibilities: Sports teams (amateur and professional), sports medicine clinics, sports training camps, private practice, and special-interest groups.

Formal Education and Specialty Training: Generally accepted credentials are a master's in nutrition or an M.D. or D.O. with a specialty in sports nutrition.

Certification and Licensing Regulations: State license is required, and board certification is preferred or required.

Universities or Associations:
American College of Sports Medicine
1440 Monroe Street
Madison, WI 53706

Salary Range: $30,000 to $100,000.

Sports Nutrition Counselor—Career Exploration Fact Sheet

A sports nutrition counselor is similar to a registered dietitian, at least superficially.

The primary functions, fundamental skills, and features are analogous, with one major exception. A counselor is not registered, and therefore functions in a narrower realm of expertise. Nonetheless, these counselors are in demand to answer general questions about nutrition and vitamins and provide nutritional guidelines to healthy clients.

Employment Possibilities:
- Health food stores and health clubs.
- A few supermarkets and restaurants employ a nutritional counselor as a consultant, part time or as a regular employee.

Formal Education and Specialty Training: A one-year or shorter diploma program (program length varies with curriculum content) to a two-year associate degree. Typical subjects studied are human anatomy and physiology, exercise physiology and its effect on nutrition, the basics of nutrition, and exercise testing and fitness program development and their relationship to nutrition. Leadership and motivational and behavioral modification techniques may also be required.

Universities or Associations:
American College of Sports Medicine
1440 Monroe Street
Madison, WI 53706

Salary Range: $12,000 to $20,000 plus, depending on your level of ambition.

Sports Psychologist—Career Exploration Fact Sheet

Primary functions:

An aerobics instructor assists a client.

- Analyze and treat psychologically based matters adversely affecting performance.
- Research human behavior in relation to health and fitness activities.
- Prepare technical papers for publication in connection with teaching at the university level.

Fundamental Skills: All revolve around interpersonal skills.

- Ability to empathize directly affects your ability to establish immediate and total client/therapist rapport.
- Ability to read the silent messages your client conveys, and a keen ear to hear exactly what your client is telling you.

Advantageous Features:

- There is a shortage of sports psychologists.
- You can structure your clientele according to your preferences.
- A very special aura of satisfaction can be shared by client and therapist, with unique personal rewards.
- Your assignments can be versatile, encompassing one-on-one and group sessions.

Questionable Features:

- If listening to a friend's problems depresses you, this may not be your best career choice.

Employment Possibilities: Special organizations (Olympics), sports clinics and hospitals, private clients (professional athletes and teams), and college campuses.

Formal Education and Specialty Training: A master's is the minimum requirement; the Ph.D. is preferred. Specialty training consists of a concentration in sports psychology.

Certification and Licensing Regulations: State licensing and board certification are the rule.

Universities or Associations:

Journal of Sports
Psychology
P.O. Box 5076
Champaign, IL 61820

Academy for the Psychology
of Sports International
2062 Arlington Avenue
Toledo, OH 43609

Salary Range: $30,000 to $50,000, with possibility for increase of up to $100,000.

Part IV—Muscle Movement

- Exercise Testing Technician
- Physical Therapist
- —Physical Therapist Assistant

Exercise Testing Technician—Career Exploration Fact Sheet (Health Risk Screening Technician)

Primary Functions:
- Administer gradation of exercise tests to establish a client's current health and fitness status.
- Interpret and analyze the complex test results to determine the client's ability to participate safely in the desired physical activity.
- Respond to and implement emergency medical procedures when appropriate.

Fundamental Skills:
- Adeptness in translating the machine output into pertinent data and applying the compiled facts to the total client assessment.
- Understanding and mastering the control of sophisticated equipment.

Advantageous Features: This career is fascinating, technologically advanced, usually fast-paced, and always challenging.

Questionable Features:

- Once your sophisticated equipment routine becomes habit, boredom can slip in, leaving you vulnerable to making mistakes that could be life-threatening if you misinterpret test results.
- Your work schedule may demand irregular hours and overtime.
- You may be under pressure to complete tests in a hurry.

Basic Equipment: Depends on many variables.

- For what facility are you testing? Local health club tests would not be as comprehensive as those for a professional athlete.
- What are you testing for? Cardiopulmonary status (lungs and heart functioning), cardiovascular endurance (heart and circulatory system effect on endurance), or both? A treadmill is fairly standard for testing cardiovascular endurance. An electrocardiogram may be used to test cardiac function. An intermittent positive pressure breathing machine (IPPB) may be needed to determine lung capacity.

Employment Possibilities: Health clubs, sports medicine clinics, university–affiliated clinics, research centers, and, with the appropriate credentials, private practice.

Formal Education and Specialty Training: The standard level of expertise and responsibilities of exercise testing technicians is difficult to establish and seems to vary from one employer to another. Although not universally accepted, a division of levels simplifies the explanation.

- Level I, which is rare, could be achieved by on-the job training. This technician does very simple testing, such as blood pressure, apical heart rate, and electro-cardiogram (EKG), on healthy clients.

- Level II technician has a two- or four-year degree with a major in exercise testing. Electrocardiograms, tread-mills, and tests of comparable difficulty are adminis-tered by these technicians.
- Note that neither level I nor level II has the authority to interpret test results. They are assistants, not actual technicians.
- Level III requires a master's, preferably a Ph.D. Specialty training generally consists of a major in exercise physiology. This is the only classification recog-nized by the American College of Sports Medicine as an exercise testing technician who has the authority to fulfill the primary functions.

Certification and Licensing Regulations: For level III, state license and board certification are required.

Universities or Associations:

American College of
  Sports Medicine
P.O. Box 1440
Indianapolis, IN 46206

American Physiological
  Society
Education Office
9650 Rockville Pike
Bethesda, MD 20014

National Athletic Health
  Association
575 East Hardy Street
Inglewood, CA 90301

Salary Range: $28,000 to $35,000.

Advancement Is Attained: By excellence of performance, superior people skills, and credentials that surpass your competitors'.

Physical Therapist—Career Exploration Fact Sheet

Primary Functions:
- Execute a therapeutic program of exercise and treatments to alleviate pain while rebuilding damaged or disabled muscles and joints to their optimum level of performance.
- Teach the client how to avoid reinjury.

Fundamental Skills:
- Ability to extract specific knowledge from your own medical background, your client's condition, and the standards of the client's sports activity is indispensable to accurate diagnosis and treatment.
- Ability to interpret and immediately apply new information is a skill worth perfecting.
- Ability to administer treatments (heat, cold, water, and sound in various forms) that complement the exercises.
- Physical coordination, strength, and patience to guide clients through exercise routines time and time again.

Advantageous Features:
- The demand for registered physical therapists is increasing.
- A superior working environment.
- The freedom to structure your own style of services.

Questionable Features:
- A client may experience recurring problems due to a biological or psychological imperfection, making recovery slow and tedious.
- Repetition of the same exercises and treatments for each client.
- Would you be vulnerable to the unwritten ethical sin of complacency? First, you assume that the client's physiological status has not changed since the last

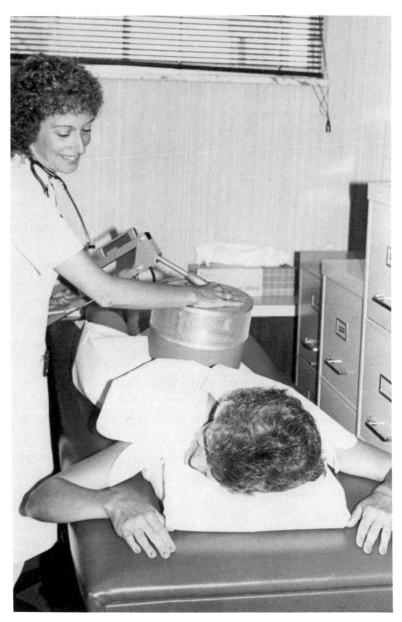

A fitness client receives ultrasound treatment.

consultation. Hence, you rely on data from previous medical records to structure the current exercise program, neglecting to reevaluate the client. Thus, you fail yourself, your client, and your profession because you did not recognize your complacency.

Basic Equipment: Various forms of heat, sound, and water (hot packs, cold compresses, whirlpool) are routinely used by physical therapists. Assistance devices (crutches, walkers, canes, braces, trapeze) and retraining equipment (parallel bars) are also common types of equipment.

Employment Possibilities:
- Private practice, with client referrals supplied by other sources (sports physician).
- Hospitals, research centers, and specialty health and fitness organizations welcome physical therapists on the rehabilitative team.

Formal Education and Specialty Training: A bachelor's degree is the minimum requirement. A master's is often recommended and is a prerequisite to advancement. Recommended specialty training consists of a concentration in sports physical therapy, with an emphasis on the musculoskeletal system and pain management. A minor in management is a definite asset.

Certification and Licensing Regulations: State license and national certification are required.

Universities or Associations:
American Physical Therapy Association
1111 North Fairfax Street
Alexandria, VA 223IF4

Salary Range: $28,000 to $38,000. Some locations much higher.

Advancement Is Attained: By demonstrated professional aptitude, formal education, and personal presentment.

Physical Therapist Assistant—Career Exploration Fact Sheet

If being a physical therapist sounds interesting but four years or more of university study does not, then being a physical therapist assistant may be a viable option.

Primary Functions: To perform the same types of tasks as the registered physical therapist under the direct supervision of a sports physician or registered physical therapist.

The fundamental skills, advantageous and questionable features, basic equipment, and employment possibilities are analogous to those of a registered physical therapist.

Formal Education and Specialty Training: Two-year associate degree with a major in physical therapy. Specialty training, if desired, would most likely take place after employment.

Universities or Associations:
American Physical Therapy Association
1111 North Fairfax Street
Alexandria, VA 2231F4

Salary Range: From $18,000 to $22,000 for an entry-level minimum.

Category A Predictable Personality Type Challenge

Is your personality type compatible with the successful professionals in this category?

Place an X in the Yes column if the characteristic listed describes you.

Place an X in the No column if the characteristic listed does not describe you.

Predictable Personality Type Challenge

Personality Type	Yes	No	Yes	No
Self-disciplined	X			
People-oriented	X			
Competitive		X		
Academically proficient		X		
Learn, retain, and apply knowledge	X			
Flexibly organized	X			
Detail-oriented	X			
Planner	X			
Negotiator	X			
Troubleshooter	X			
Set realistic goals	X			
Motivator	X			
Concentration	X			
Independent	X			
Prioritize	X			
Total Points*	+4			

* 3 Yes = 1 point

You must answer Yes to 3 personality types to accumulate 1 point. Those answered No, and less than 3 Yes, = 0 points.

Additional health and fitness career choices you may wish to research:

• Preventive and Rehabilitative Exercise Specialist
• Preventive and Rehabilitative Exercise Program Director

CATEGORY B—HEALTH AND FITNESS INSTRUCTORS

- Coach—Team and Private Client
- Athletic Trainer
- Physical Education Teacher
- Fitness Specialty Instructor

Each of these four classifications of instructors teaches people a special sports or fitness skill (aerobic dancing) or series of skills and techniques (tennis or swimming).

Coach—Team and Private Client—Career Exploration Fact Sheet

Primary Functions:
- Teach clients game-winning maneuvers and strategies for a particular sport or fitness activity.
- Supervise and routinely assess each client's skills.
- Work individually with clients, helping each to master and perfect physical skills and techniques related to the sport.
- Meet with clients' trainers and assistant coaches to gain their input.
- Plan, organize, and schedule training sessions and games.
- Post the starting line-up, and substitute participants when appropriate.
- Recruit and select team members whose physical and personal attributes complement one another and facilitate teamwork (especially college and professional athletes).
- Be aware of your league's scouting trends and how your

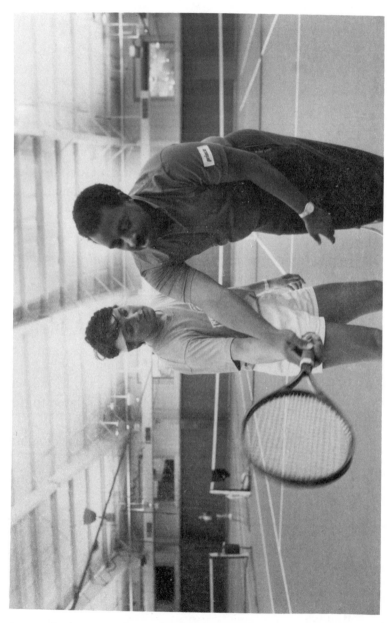

A tennis pro coaches a fitness client.

team members are assessed by other scouts (especially college and professional athletes).

- Hold press conferences and media interviews, issue press releases (especially college and professional athletes).

Fundamental Skills:
- Ability to deal tactfully with people and establish rapport with clients.
- An eye for recognizing unpolished talent.
- Excellent organizational and communication skills.
- Comprehensive knowledge of the sport's rules, strategies, and techniques.
- Ability to teach, lead, and motivate clients to achieve peak performance.
- Ability to gather and interpret facts on the competition and incorporate these into your game plan.

Advantageous Features:
- A prestigious and highly visible position, in which you remain close to or part of the action at all times.
- A variety of responsibilities prevents boredom.

Questionable Features:
- Extremely competitive at the top (college, professional), with job security very precarious.
- You travel with the team during training and the season.
- The schedule and the pressure to succeed are relentless.

Basic Equipment: Determined by the sport(s) you coach.

Employment Possibilities: Elementary through high schools, universities, amateur and professional teams or individuals, special events (recreational to world championships), recreational leagues, and community programs.

Formal Education and Specialty Training: Bachelor of science is standard, with a master's in physical education highly recommended. Specialty training in sports management with a concentration in coaching is a definite asset. Typical curriculum studies focus on understanding the human growth and development cycle (from infant through senior citizen) and its impact on performance in the fitness activity. First aid, safety practices and techniques, injury prevention, and legal liabilities are valuable information. A working knowledge of the physical, psychological, emotional, and intellectual values of the sport is necessary before you can instill this knowledge in each client. Experience in the sport you wish to coach is essential.

Certification Programs: Coaches' certification programs are not standardized. Each state establishes its own standards. Some states require certification. Other states permit only certified educators to coach.

Universities or Associations:

National Youth Sports Coaches Association
1509 North Military Trail
West Palm Beach, FL 33409

National High School Athletic Coaches Association
3423 East Silver Spring Boulevard
Ocala, FL 32670

Salary Range: Wide range, depending on your formal goals —$16,000 to $50,000. College and professional coaches earn excellent salaries; $100,000 and even $200,000 is not unheard of, plus subsidiary income from advertisements, endorsing products, television or radio talk shows, oral presentations, or summer sports camps. A word of caution: college and professional coach vacancies are few and are often filled before the vacancy becomes public knowledge.

Advancement Is Attained: By going from assistant coach to head coach; however, this is very difficult to achieve for college and professional coaches.

Athletic Trainer—Career Exploration Fact Sheet

Primary Functions:
- Assist the client in choosing appropriate gear for the sport, usually with input from the coach and equipment manager.
- Apply protective or corrective devices to your client when needed.
- Develop and monitor your clients' training and conditioning programs before they participate in their sport.
- Follow the sports physician's orders by designing, monitoring, and adjusting clients' rehabilitative program.
- Implement an injury-prevention regimen.
- Initiate on-site emergency treatment as ordered by the sports physician.
- Maintain the athletic training area, assess for safety, and remove or correct any risk factors.

Fundamental Skills:
- Function effectively as a team member.
- Understand the sport in order to choose appropriate gear.
- Understand human anatomy and physiology to help prevent injuries or to rehabilitate injured clients.

Advantageous Features:
- You are a major influence on your clients' attitudes.
- You play a valuable role in keeping teams intact or an independent client able to play.

Questionable Features:
- You might have to travel to meets with the team or client.
- You frequently work irregular hours and overtime.
- The higher your rank, the more pressure you must endure.

Basic Equipment: Determined by your sport specialty.

Employment Possibilities: Educational institutions and anywhere professional and amateur sports are played. Less obvious are hospitals, clinics, and research centers.

Formal Education and Specialty Training: Bachelor of science in physical education, with a certified program in athletic training, is usually expected. A typical curriculum may consist of: human anatomy and physiology, psychology, growth and development, first aid, advanced first aid, athletic injuries I and II, biomechanics, and a sports practicum in athletic training.

Certification Programs: National certification examination is required.

Universities or Associations:

National Athletic Trainers Association
112 South Pitt Street
Greenville, NC 27834

Athletic Trainers Association and Certification Board
638 West Durarte Road
Arcadia, CA 91006

Salary Range: $25,000. Professional team trainers earn significantly more.

Advancement Is Attained: By working your way up the ladder, and by advanced education.

Physical Education Teacher—Career Exploration Fact Sheet

Primary Functions:

- Nurture the physiological, mental, emotional, and psychological development of your clients in a wide range of sports.
- Creatively design physical education classes to accommodate the clients' level of skill and stage of development (usually school-age).

- Evaluate each client's baseline abilities and project realistic optimum potential.
- Individualize training sessions when teaching a skill.
- Monitor the achievements of each client, intervening with supportive encouragement and direction when necessary. Particular attention should be directed to underachievers, introverts, and the physically or mentally handicapped, to help them to reach their peak performance.
- File reports of accidents and injuries, including follow-up, to protect all interested parties from legal liabilities.

Fundamental Skills:

- Understand the stages of human growth and development and the skills required to master a sport before evaluating a client's current and projected abilities.
- Create a fun-to-learn atmosphere for everyone.
- Know your clients' personality types and observe their performance.
- Accurately observe accidents and injuries, report the details, and interview the victim(s) or witnesses to acquire the needed facts for your report.
- Be knowledgeable of your equipment needs, initial cost, depreciation, and repair.
- Be a good communicator, and have patience to work with the novice.

Advantageous Features:

- You are a respected community leader.
- You have an opportunity to help clients achieve new heights of maturation and achievement.
- You can be a confidant to a client in need, wisely counseling on sensitive matters.

Questionable Features:

- You must be adept at all sports, not just one.

- You must be able to work with several skill levels within one class. This is very challenging.

Basic Equipment: Determined by the sport being taught.

Employment Possibilities: Schools (elementary through college), clubs (private and public), social agencies, and community programs.

Formal Education and Specialty Training: Bachelor of science in physical education, with a master's preferred. You are urged to supplement your major with electives in business administration, recreation, and communication. Sports experience is an asset. Internship as a physical education instructor is usually required. A typical curriculum includes courses in communication skills, humanities and the fine arts, mathematics, biology, history, and social and natural science.

Certification Programs: State certification for teaching is usually required.

Universities or Associations:
American Alliance for Physical Education,
   Health, Recreation, and Dance
1900 Association Drive
Reston, VA 22070

Salary Range: $16,000 to $30,000.

Advancement Is Attained: Usually by changing your status to coach or trainer and specializing in one sport.

Fitness Specialty Instructors—Career Exploration Fact Sheet

Learning resource centers and bookstores have many books on the numerous types of fitness, recreation, or sports specialty instructor positions and the training required for each. These specialty fitness programs encompass all age groups and all skill levels from purely recreational to professional.

- Some fitness specialty instructors use dance (aerobics, jazzercise, and dancercise) as their teaching medium.
- Others concentrate on a specific skill taught as part of an aerobically sound exercise; karate is an example.
- Perhaps a particular sport interests you. Tennis, racquetball, handball, water skiing, snow skiing (downill or cross country), running, and swimming are a few of the many sports taught to the general public by specialty instructors.
- Some clients seek the physical endurance programs. Iron man triathlon and survival are two highly publicized events.

All facets of the Fact Sheet are very similar. Hence, for simplicity, fitness specialty instructor is addressed as one career with several disciplines.

Primary Functions:
- Establish the client's baseline of fitness and skill level.
- Determine the client's innate abilities and anticipate the optimum level of performance.
- Design a fitness program to meet the client's specific needs within these parameters.
- Implement motivational, instructional, and behavioral modification techniques when appropriate, to nurture healthy habits.

Fundamental Skills:
- You must be physically adept, knowledgeable, and capable of teaching your chosen activity.
- You must be acutely aware of injury liability problems and work to avert them through techniques and programs specially designed for the age group, skill, and development level you instruct.

- You should be flexible, approachable, enthusiastic, observant, and a skilled communicator.
- You must have the strength to withstand the physical demands of your work.
- You must look like a fitness specialty instructor.

Advantageous Features:
- Currently, the demand for qualified fitness specialty instructors exceeds the supply.
- Every conceivable sports and fitness activity slides into this category.
- This is a unique opportunity to teach any age group (infants through senior citizens), on any level of intensity (low to high impact), in any skill level (novice, intermediate, or advanced), with any special needs (handicapped, to recovering from illness or injury).

Questionable Features:
- Your schedule can be irregular to meet company or client expectations.
- If you travel to your clients' homes or worksites, driving may impose an extra expense.
- You must be physically active and promote a positive emotional atmosphere at all times.
- You must set standards appropriate to the group you plan to instruct, and then adapt a program that meets those standards. If you choose a general aerobics class in a health club, you must maintain a careful balance, keeping all participants involved. Care must be exercised not to bypass the underachiever nor neglect to challenge the overachiever.

Basic Equipment: Appropriate to the fitness activity you teach.

Employment Possibilities: Health resorts, camps (special,

A trainer guides a fitness client work on the Nautilus machines.

An aerobics instructor conducts class.

A trainer assists a fitness client with free weights.

public, private), schools, health clubs, spas, gymnasiums, independent businesses, and retirement centers.

Formal Education and Specialty Training: Educational preparation and training depend on the type of instruction. Your curriculum could include such subjects as these: total fitness with an emphasis on cardiovascular fitness, human anatomy, physiology of muscle movement, strength, endurance, and flexibility, basic cardiopulmonary resuscitation (CPR), first aid for injuries and medical emergencies, injury prevention, fitness program development concentrating on special-needs clients (handicapped, senior citizens, recovering heart attack victims), managerial techniques, and legal, moral, and ethical issues as they affect your professional performance. Nutrition and weight control are probably integrated into the curriculum.

Certification Programs: There is a broad spectrum of employment credentials, from the basic workshop/seminar certification, which requires less than one year of training, to the Ph.D. degree. Although you may be able to obtain employment without certification, for your own protection you should consult your governing association. If your tennis association recommends or requires certification, comply. Often, less than a week is required for the review workshop-seminar and certification examination. Certification in basic first aid and CPR is highly recommended but not required. These certifications can usually be obtained through the local Red Cross unit. National certification programs, often produced by the specialty association, may test your theoretical knowledge in these subjects: evaluating a client's total fitness; developing an exercise program to meet clients' fitness needs and personal goals; human anatomy; exercise physiology; cardiovascular fitness; CPR; first aid; calculation of body composition (percentage of muscle versus body fat); and nutrition for weight control. You may be tested on legal, moral, and ethical obligations. You should know instruction techniques and be able to perform an on-site evaluation of your client's total abilities. Creativity must be incorporated into your exercise routine. You will probably be required to demonstrate your instructional expertise, focusing on proper exercise technique. Certification requires a written and a practical exam. Some certification processes require an oral exam.

Universities or Associations:
American Association of Fitness
   Directors in Business and Industry
700 Anderson Hill Road
Purchase, NY 10577

Salary Range: $16,000 to $40,000, depending on credentials and employer. Large corporations usually pay more than privately owned businesses.

Advancement Is Attained: By continuing education and perfecting your expertise.

References for Review

Careers in Physical Education and Sports
American Alliance Publication Sales
1900 Association Drive
Reston, VA 22091

Category B Predictable Personality Type Challenge

Is your personality type compatible with successful professionals in this category?

Place an X in the Yes column if the characteristic listed describes you.

Place an X in the No column if the characteristic listed does not describe you.

Predictable Personality Type Challenge

Personality Type	Yes	No	Yes	No
Coordinated	X			
Love sports	X			
Physically healthy	X			
Creative	X			
Extrovert	X			
Vivacious	X			
Highly charged	X			
Excellent people skills	X			
Motivator	X			
Happy most of the time	X			
Empathetic	X			
Communicator	X			
Group Leader	X			
Patient	X			
Organized		X		
Total Points*	+4			

* 3 Yes = 1 point

You must answer Yes to 3 personality types to accumulate 1 point. Those answered No, and less than 3 Yes, = 0 points.

CATEGORY C—DESTINATION CHIEF EXECUTIVE OFFICER (CEO)

- Athletic Administrator
- Information Coordinator–
  Public Relations Coordinator
- Sporting Events Coordinator
- Sports Program Coordinator
  - General Public Sports Program Coordinator
  - Children's Fitness Program Coordinator
  - Public Agency Fitness Program Coordinator

Destination Chief Executive Officer covers only a few of the many options for managerial employment in the health and fitness zone.

Athletic Administrator—Career Exploration Fact Sheet

Athletic administrators may have different titles, depending on the organization they manage.

- Athletic administrator refers to a director of high schools or universities.
- Commissioner denotes the CEO of a professional sports league.
- Other titles are director of player development and director of minor league operations.

The primary functions may change to accommodate a particular organizations's requirements. What follows is a broad description of high school or university athletic administrators.

Primary Functions:
- Research, develop, and supervise high school and university athletic curriculums.
- Monitor athletic-related operations: business office, public information, schedules, budget, transportation; monitor support system activities and meetings (coaches, trainers, equipment managers); regulate sports arena, and coordinate intramural sporting events.

Fundamental Skills:
- Planning, organizing, troubleshooting, and communicating are essential.
- Ability to judge when one of your support staff needs a little less pressure or a little more encouragement.
- Understanding the impact of athletic events on the student and the educational system.

Advantageous Features:
- Opportunity to observe the gradual maturation and perfection of talents.
- Administrators are highly visible and are often credited with the success of their clients.

Questionable Features:
- Your work schedule is often hectic, involving overtime and weekend commitments.
- You could be the scapegoat when your clients fail.

Employment Possibilities: High schools and institutions of higher learning; professional sports organizations.

Formal Education and Specialty Training: Customarily a bachelor's in sports management or athletic administration is mandatory. A concentration in sports studies with on-site instructional fitness activities is a definite asset.

Universities or Associations:
National Association of Athletic,
    Marketing and Development Directors
Athletic Department
University of Michigan
1000 South State Street
Ann Arbor, MI 48109

National Interscholastic   National Association of
    Athletic   Collegiate Directors of
    Administrators   Athletics
    Association   21330 Center Ridge Road
P.O. Box 20626   Cleveland, OH 44116
11724 Plaza Circle
Kansas City, MO 64195

Salary Range: $20,000 to $40,000. Commissioners can command salaries of $100,000, but the position is rare and elusive.

Advancement Is Attained: By working up through the ranks, backed by an educational degree.

Information Coordinator—Public Relations Coordinator
Career Exploration Fact Sheet

Virtually any health and fitness service or business can utilize the services of a public relations coordinator. Information coordinators of colleges and universities are highlighted because of their analogous relationship to public relations coordinators in professional and amateur sports. (See *Media Talk* for General Public Relations Personnel— Career Exploration Fact Sheet.)

Primary Functions:
- To direct all actions and activities that will project a positive image of the sport, team members, college, or

organization, thereby generating public interest in the sport and the university or team.

- Provide noteworthy statistics appropriate to the sport (win/lose record, field goal distance, earned run average, free-throw percentage, average points per game).
- Schedule and coordinate client, coach, personal, or other appearances with the media to release information.
- Send press releases to newspapers, television, radio.
- Attend meetings and activities promoting public interest in the institution or organization, clients, and teams.
- Establish communications with the manager of the team or fitness organization to discuss potential problems and exchange information.
- Manage press box activities such as seating arrangements, right of admission, and data for media use.

Fundamental Skills:

- Communication (written, spoken, silent) is of paramount importance.
- Ability to organize, plan, conduct, and participate in meetings.
- Ability to handle high-pressure situations.
- Ability to establish rapport with others is a prerequisite to effective delegating, negotiating, and compromising on sensitive issues.

Advantageous Features:

- You are the center of attention. The reputation of the organization and its members depends on your ability to project a positive image to the public.
- The individual team members, general public, media, team manager, and various organizations and associations all seek your wisdom and input.

Questionable Features:
- These areas are overcrowded and continuing to experience a population increase annually, without a substantial increase in vacancies. Availability of public relations coordinator jobs at the professional team level is minimal.
- Your schedule is hectic, with overtime, irregular hours, and deadlines fairly common.

Employment Possibilities: Limited to institutions of higher learning and amateur and professional sports.

Formal Education and Specialty Training: Bachelor of science with major in communications, emphasis in journalism or radio/television, electives in public relations, physical education, and sports studies is the recommended preparation. While still in high school, saturate your curriculum with computer science, public speaking, journalism, and photography.

Universities or Associations:
College Sports Information
   Directors of America
Campus Box 114
Texas A & I University
Kingsville, TX 78363

Salary Range: $22,000 to $32,000.

Advancement Is Attained: Usually by proven expertise and educational status. Advancement into professional sports extremely competitive.

Sporting Events Coordinator—Career Exploration Fact Sheet

Primary Functions:
- To be certain that the physical plan of the facility can accommodate the sporting event.

- To coordinate all the support systems of a sporting event, insuring uninterrupted action.

Fundamental Skills:
- Must understand the intricacies of an event. The Boston Marathon organizer must consider start and finish line, strategic placement of checkpoints, and the support staff required. A bowling tournament organizer would have other concerns.
- Must be skilled in communications, planning, public relations, troubleshooting, motivating staff, and managing.

Advantageous Features:
- You are always in the middle of the action.
- There is continuous social interaction and mental stimulation.

Questionable Features:
- Your work schedule can be hectic, involving overtime and weekend commitments.
- The career may be seasonal in some states.

Employment Possibilities: Any building, area, or place where sporting events occur (stadiums, racetracks, auditoriums, coliseums).

Formal Education and Specialty Training: Educational requirements are not standardized. Vacancies at the top are sure to be filled by persons with a bachelor of science in sports management, with preference given to a master's.

Universities or Associations:
National Association of Athletic
  Marketing and Development Directors
Athletic Department
University of Michigan
1000 South State Street
Ann Arbor, MI 48109

Salary Range: $20,000 to $40,000.
Advancement Is Attained: By working up through the ranks. Internship during college and entry-level experience enhance the promotional process.

Sports Program Coordinator—Career Exploration Fact Sheet

- *General public sports program coordinators* plan, implement, and supervise all components of health and fitness programs (primarily adult recreational).

- *Children's fitness program coordinators* plan, implement, and supervise all components of health and fitness programs (primarily working with children, special needs, or recreational).

- *Public agency fitness program coordinators* plan, implement, and supervise all components of recreational fitness programs at public agencies.

Primary Functions:
- Evaluate the instructors you supervise.
- Monitor fitness events and determine appropriateness of purpose and presentation.

Fundamental Skills:
- Knowledge of the fitness activity you supervise.
- Knowledge of each instructor's intrinsic qualities to insure quality control.
- Communication skills.
- General management skills of planning, organizing, and troubleshooting.

Advantageous Features:
- You are an indispensable part of the activity, needed and admired by all.
- You are drawn into the fun times of the instructors and clients.

The manager of a health club has a complex role.

Questionable Features:
- Your schedule is fast-paced.
- You will be subject to external stimuli from the noise and unavoidable interruptions generated during activity.
- Clients may question or criticize your decisions.

Employment Possibilities:
- Resorts, health clubs, spas, civic and community organizations, and children's camps. For public agency program coordinators, churches, YWCA, YMCA, scouting organizations, and correctional institutions.

Formal Education and Specialty Training: An associate or bachelor of science degree with a major in recreation or physical education is highly regarded. An emphasis in a specialty is advised. Experience with groups, a business background, and teaching experience are helpful.

Universities or Associations:

National Association of
    Athletic, Marketing and
    Development Directors
    Athletic Department
    University of Michigan
    1000 South State Street
    Ann Arbor, MI 48109

National Interscholastic
    Athletic Administrators
    Association
11724 Plaza Circle
Kansas City, MD 64195

National Association of
    Collegiate Directors of
    Athletics
21330 Center Ridge Road
Cleveland, OH 44116

Salary Range: $16,000 and up.

Advancement Is Attained: By experience, demonstrated ability, and advanced education.

Category C Predictable Personality Type Challenge

Is your personality type compatible with the successful professionals in this category?

Place an X in the Yes column if the characteristic listed describes you.

Place an X in the No column if the characteristic listed does not describe you.

Predictable Personality Type Challenge				
Personality Type	Yes	No	Yes	No
Communication	X			
Public Speaking		X		
Organization	X			
Compromise	X			
Delegate	X			
Negotiate	X			
Establish rapport	X			
Plan	X			
Conduct meetings	X			
Leadership	X			
Troubleshooting	X			
Supervising	X			
Approachability		X		
Motivating	X			
Independent	X			
Total Points*	+4			

* 3 Yes = 1 point

You must answer Yes to 3 personality types to accumulate 1 point. Those answered No, and less than 3 Yes, = 0 points.

CATEGORY D—HEALTH AND FITNESS
—MEDIA TALK

- Sports Broadcaster
- Sportswriter
- Sports Photographer
- Public Relations Personnel
- Sports Statistician

Media Talk is a broad term for any method of message transference that completes a cycle from a sender to a receiver. In the realm of health and fitness, the receiver collects, interprets, and analyzes the message and then returns a message in the form of feedback. The sender's message can take many forms, direct or indirect, deliberate or accidental, planned or spontaneous. The messages may also be in different forms of delivery such as spoken, written, or silent (otherwise known as body language).

To perform proficiently in the area of media talk, it is of paramount importance that you acquire or perfect communication skills. Stop and think about yourself for a few minutes.

- Can you quickly survey your audience, observing their silent reactions (receiver) to your message (sender)? If you are failing to achieve the desired results, can you recognize that fact and immediately adjust your voice intonation, vocabulary, or personal presentation to achieve listener involvement?
- Are you a keen listener? Do you hear, comprehend, and

confirm the sender's message by paraphrasing and feedback?

- Are you capable of observing for specific facts, then documenting exactly what you witnessed?
- Are you a dramatic speaker as you announce the winning touchdown or a grand slam home run? Oral communication skills are of particular importance to the sports broadcaster, who must with words alone create a vivid visual image of events as they unfold.
- Can you capture the "magic play" of the game on film? A sports photographer must thoroughly grasp the use of silent talk to capture the best moments on film.
- Are you a word wizard? The sportswriter must have an excellent command of the English language to make the game come to life.
- Public relations personnel are vulnerable to over-exposure in any of the three spheres of communication, oral, written, and silent. Is your silent talk really silent, or are you a babbling brook? Do your friends know your thoughts before you express them? Can a stranger accurately predict your response to a particular question? Whenever you deliver an oral presentation, your total personal presentment will be scrutinized by the viewer. Hence, to sell your product or service, you must appeal to your listeners' sense of need and convince them that their search has ended. When marketing on this level, you can memorize your copy before your appearance, but your silent talk is not as easily regulated. At all times, be acutely aware of your responses, reactions, and interactions. Silent talk leaves a lasting impression that may have a stronger impact than any words you could speak.

Your demonstrated interpersonal and social expertise will strongly affect your ability to succeed as a media talk professional. Your persistence to elicit accurate facts, especially during interviews, and perform your research flawlessly are important assets. Communication skills are tools of the trade for media talk professionals.

Sports Broadcaster—Career Exploration Fact Sheet

Primary functions:

- The sports broadcaster is responsible for complete game coverage on television or radio, announcing play-by-play action as it occurs.
- Preparations for broadcasting are time-consuming. Perhaps you attend a press conference or interview an athlete, coach, trainer, or manager. Your personal involvement bolsters your credibility as a broadcaster knowledgeable of the rules, techniques, and strategies of the sport.

Fundamental Skills:

- The broadcaster must have excellent verbal communication skills. An extensive vocabulary is not necessary, but the ability to stimulate listener involvement by projecting excitement, enthusiasm, and a realistic image of the event is vital to success.
- The broadcaster must know and be able to interpret the rules of the game. Unlike the sportswriter, who can rewrite his copy as often as necessary, the broadcaster has only a split second to react and send a resounding message.
- A pleasing speaking voice is essential.
- Writing ability is essential for sports broadcasters who

review the news of the day, as they are responsible for composing their own copy.

- The ability to imprint your own style by adding amusing anecdotes or interesting commentary is a winning asset.

Advantageous Features:
- Television sports broadcasting is considered a glamorous career, highly visible and highly regarded.
- You meet the professional and amateur athletes, trainers, coaches, managers, and agents.

Questionable Features:
- Sports broadcasting careers, especially in television, are scarce.
- You face irregular and overtime hours, overnight travel, bright lights, and crowd noise. Deadlines are tight, and the pace is hectic.

Basic Equipment: Technical radio and television equipment.

Employment Possibilities: Compensation by the radio or television station and the team for which you broadcast.

Formal Education and Specialty Training: Bachelor of science in liberal arts, communications, or journalism. Technical schools offer intensive courses in sports broadcasting. Sports experience and knowledge are critical to perfecting your expertise. An internship can be valuable.

Universities and Associations:

National Association of
 Broadcasters
1771 N Street NW
Washington, DC 20036

National Sportscasters and
 Sportswriters Association
P.O. Drawer 559
Salisbury, NC 28114

Salary Range: $18,000 in a small radio station to $100,000 in network television.

Advancement Is Attained: By the slow climb of proven excellence and education, unless you are a former or retired professional athlete. Television and even professional sports broadcasting is extremely competitive.

Sportswriter—Career Exploration Fact Sheet

Primary Functions: Writing, researching, and editing for the print media on sports events, issues, and participants.

Fundamental Skills:
- Ability to give an account of sports events as they unfold, analyzing, predicting, and explaining what has happened or could happen.
- Knowledge of all the latest sports news of interest to the general public.

Advantageous Features:
- You meet the professional and amateur athletes, trainers, coaches, managers, and agents.
- Your work receives immediate attention from the public as they read the details of the sport you cover.

Questionable Features:
- You face irregular and overtime hours, overnight travel, bright lights, and crowd noise. Deadlines are tight, and the pace is hectic.
- Free-lancers can earn higher pay than permanent personnel, but face more hassles and job insecurity.

Employment Possibilities: Any form of print media, usually commencing with school or college newspapers. Small-town newspapers may receive sports coverage from the wire services. Sportswriters of major newspapers may specialize in one sport. You might write magazine articles or books about your sport.

Formal Education and Specialty Training: Bachelor of science in communication arts, journalism, or liberal arts is required. Curriculum should include writing, grammar, humanities, sports, and photography. Sports experience and a sportswriting internship are valuable.

Universities or Associations:
American Council on Education
  for Journalism
563 Essex Court
Deerfield, IL 60015

Salary Range: $16,000 to $30,000 plus. Books and magazine articles generate additional income.

Advancement Is Attained: By formal education and proven expertise.

Sports Photographer—Career Exploration Fact Sheet

Primary Functions: To capture and preserve on film special moments of a sports event. Photographs of the participants' emotional responses and winning movements vividly recapture the action as it happened. A detailed story can be told in pictures, still shots or live action.

Fundamental Skills: Ability in all phases of photography and knowledge of your sport. You must be aware of the superior plays as well as the bloopers, to give the audience the total picture.

Advantageous Features:
- You meet the professional and amateur athletes, trainers, coaches, managers, and agents.
- Your work receives immediate attention from the public as they view your live action shots of the event on television or see the stills in the newspaper.

Questionable Features:
- You face irregular and overtime hours, overnight travel, bright lights, and crowd noise. Deadlines are tight, and the pace is hectic.

Basic Equipment: Photography equipment. Your employer will dictate the degree of sophisticated equipment you must use.

Employment Possibilities:

- On staff at a newspaper or magazine.
- Free-lance, by offering your services directly to the client.
- A sports team, an individual, the sponsor of the event, or the product or service business promoting the event.

Formal Education and Specialty Training: Prerequisites are not standardized. A college degree majoring in sports and photography gives you an edge on the competition. A portfolio representative of the quality and type of photographs you take is mandatory. Sports experience and knowledge are valuable assets.

Universities and Associations:

Photographic Society of America
P.O. Box 1266
Reseda, CA 91335

Salary Range: Difficult to establish.

Advancement Is Attained: By proven excellence and advanced specialty training.

Public Relations Personnel—Career Exploration Fact Sheet

Primary Functions: To create and project a positive image of the business you represent, increase visibility, raise profits, and insure public awareness of new or improved services or products.

Fundamental Skills:

- Excellent written, spoken, and silent communication skills.
- Ability to conduct market research and then follow up with target advertising.

The public relations department uses the bulletin board to promote club activities.

- Understanding of profit and loss sheets and ability to plan cost-effective marketing.
- Ability to establish rapport and convey a trustworthy image.
- You should be independent, self-motivated, and inventive.

Advantageous Features:
- This career offers an independent, self-structured work atmosphere.
- Opportunities for personal appearances before the media as well as one-on-one meetings with clients.

Questionable Features:
- The hours can be long, especially during the promotion of a new product, service, or special event.
- You must always be at your best.

Employment Possibilities: Any business or industry large enough to require a public relations staff member to promote its image.

Formal Education and Specialty Training: Commonly recommended is a bachelor of science with a major in communications and a concentration in public relations and fitness studies. High school courses in computers, graphics, public speaking, journalism, and photography offer a good foundation.

Universities and Associations: Consult your academic adviser for universities in your vicinity.

Salary Range: $17,000 to $23,000.

Advancement Is Attained: By experience and education.

Sports Statistician—Career Exploration Fact Sheet

Primary Functions: To gather, analyze, and interpret pertinent mathematical data to a team coach, manager, owner, or the front office.

Fundamental Skills:
- An attention span long enough to translate tedious, detailed statistics into concise, understandable data.
- You should be detail-oriented and adept with numbers, have a good command of language, and have good communication skills.

Advantageous Features: This is the domain of the mathematical whiz.

Questionable Features: High-speed technology has placed sports statistician on the endangered careers list. Coaches or management personnel either accept the responsibility themselves or hire a part-time or free-lance statistician as needed.

Employment Possibilities: Sports teams.

Formal Education and Specialty Training: A solid background in mathematics and computer studies is advisable.

Universities and Associations: Consult specific sports organizations.

Salary Range: $12,000 to $16,000.

Category D Predictable Personality Type Challenge

Is your personality type compatible with the successful professionals in this category?

Place an X in the Yes column if the characteristic listed describes you.

Place an X in the No column if the characteristic listed does not describe you.

Predictable Personality Type Challenge

Personality Type	Yes	No	Yes	No
Excellent communicator	X			
Observant	X			
Evaluation	X			
Public appearances	X			
People skills	X			
Adaptable	X			
Flexible	X			
Know yourself	X			
Persistent	X			
Accurate	X			
Accept criticism	X			
Self-confident	X			
Sense of humor		X		
Assertive	X			
Extrovert	X			
Total Points*	+4			

* 3 Yes = 1 point

You must answer Yes to 3 personality types to accumulate 1 point. Those answered No, and less than 3 Yes, = 0 points.

Category E—RETAIL SALES CAREER CHOICES

Health and Fitness Retail Sales—Career Exploration Fact Sheet

Retail sales covers a broad spectrum of enterprises and levels of management, ranging from the sole employee of a small, independent store responsible for the shop during a given shift, to the chief executive officer of an empire like Nautilus exercise equipment.

Primary Functions:
- A small firm would most likely concentrate on development, marketing, and promotion of product lines to increase profit.
- A larger firm would tend to concentrate on people management, market analysis, quality control, and the bottom line—profit and loss.

Fundamental Skills:
- Ability to identify your target market and thoroughly understand all aspects of your product.
- General business knowledge.
- Good communication skills and the ability to listen carefully to consumer complaints and compliments. Both complaints and compliments should be incorporated into the design and production of a product to satisfy market needs and generate sales.

Advantageous and Questionable Features: You are in charge of the operation. Your business style will determine your skyrocketing success or your plummeting defeat.

Employment Possibilities: Any and every business that deals in health and fitness-related entities is a viable candidate. Dance studios, health clubs, resorts, country clubs, racquet clubs, health food stores, sporting goods stores, sports or fitness-oriented clothing stores. You have three basic business structures to consider.
- A private entrepreneurship is owned and operated by one person. Top-level management usually has less earning potential than those employed by a huge corpo-

ration. On the other hand, managers for independent businesses often reap intangible benefits. The owner may show appreciation with bonuses. The atmosphere is more controllable, flexible, less tense, and offers more freedom if you and the owner have good rapport.

• A franchiser purchases and operates a store from the business developer, such as McDonalds. As a fanchise owner, you gain certain rights and accept certain responsibilities established by the corporation.

• A chain store is one of many stores owned, operated, and controlled by the governing body, usually a corporation. A large corporation with many chain stores offers employment opportunities on all levels: clerk, to assistant department manager, to department manager; to branch manager, to district manager, to state manager, to regional manager, to national headquarters management.

Formal Education and Specialty Training: Logically, the more you know about a product, and the more business sense you possess, the faster you will realize success. If your goal is chief executive officer of a major corporation, a bachelor of science is expected, with a master's given preference. Personal experience with the product you represent is an asset. A degree in the sport or area to which the product line is related and business management experience are also helpful.

Salary Range: $16,000 to $100,000.

Advancement Is Attained: By proven expertise and formal education.

Category E Predictable Personality Type Challenge

Is your personality type compatible with successful professionals in this category?

Place an X in the Yes column if the characteristic listed describes you.

Place an X in the No column if the characteristic listed does not describe you.

Predictable Personality Type Challenge				
Personality Type	Yes	No	Yes	No
Independence	X			
People skills	X			
Verbal skills	X			
Convincing attitude		X		
Business sense	X			
Personal presentment	X			
Self-confidence	X			
Good listener	X			
Patient	X			
Approachability	X			
Integrity	X			
Self-motivated	X			
Extrovert		X		
Decisive	X			
Troubleshooter	X			
Total Points*	+4			

* 3 Yes = 1 point

You must answer Yes to 3 personality types to accumulate 1 point. Those answered No, and less than 3 Yes, = 0 points.

SELECT YOUR FAVORITE CAREER CHOICES

You are now ready to fill in your Rating Sheets and discover your favorite career choices.

To discover your favorite career choices, review the five category introduction sheets and rank the categories in order of preference.

Category A: Health and Fitness Advisers, page 9.

Category B: Health and Fitness Instructors, page 35.

Category C: Managerial Opportunities, page 51.

Category D: Health and Fitness Media Talk, page 61.

Category E: Health and Fitness Retail Sales, page 71.

Flip to the end of your favorite category and take the corresponding Predictable Personality Type Challenge.

The Predictable Personality Type Challenge is a checklist of personality types who are usually successful in this category. These are not the only types that have proven successful, nor have all the successful personality types been listed. You will always find successful persons whose type seems incompatible with the "typical" personality. If the questions did not reveal your personality type, try to discern if there is a significant difference between yourself and the suggested type. If you are reasonably sure that you would like the type of work the career would demand and could handle the problems that might be expected, you probably have a successful personality type for that career.

If the category of health and fitness careers still appeals to you, reread the Fact Sheets of the career choices in which you have even a probable interest. List the ones you like best in that category.

Using the same procedure, reread the introduction sheets of the other categories, take the corresponding Predictable Personality Type Challenge at the end of each category, read the Career Exploration Fact Sheets, and list the career choices most appealing to you.

After you have reviewed all five categories, return to your first choice. Read each of your career choice Career Exploration Fact Sheets and evaluate your degree of *genuine* interest as:

- very interested (4 points)
- moderately interested (3 points)
- slightly interested (2 points)
- possibly interested (1 point)

Preliminary Career Exploration Rating Sheet

Career Choice	Points	Degree of Interest	Principal Reason for Interest
Category A:			
medical exercise physiologist	3	moderately	enjoy research and exercise
exercise testing technician	2	slightly	mechanical aptitude lacking
sports medical biomechanics	1	possibly	mildly interested in biomechanics
sports psychologist	4	very	human behavior is fascinating
Category D:			
sportswriter	4	very	love sports and writing

Prepare one Career Exploration Rating Sheet for each career on your chart. Use one sheet of paper per career.

Sports Psychologist
Career Exploration Rating Sheet

Section—	Points	Comments
interest—very	+4	human behavior is fascinating

Separate careers according to interest rating, placing all the careers you think could be very interesting (4 points) in one pile. Cross-stack beneath the very interesting careers, the careers you rate as moderately interesting (3 points). Label this stack prospective favorite career choices. Likewise stack your slightly interesting (2 points) and possibly interesting (1 point) choices and set them aside for the time being.

Program your personal data bank for successful career selection. Place one of the Rating Sheets from your prospective favorite career choices in front of you.

Sports Psychologist
Career Exploration Rating Sheet

Section—	Points	Comments
interest very	+4	human behavior is fascinating

Refer to that career choice's Fact Sheet. Scrutinize every detail of this career. Answer the following questions honestly. You will notice that "Maybe" is not offered as an acceptable response. At this time, you must make your best career choice(s). If after the rating sheet is complete you are unsure of the results, you can always redo the rating sheet.

Career Questions: No = 0. Yes = +1. Total points = 5.

A. Would you enjoy routinely performing the primary function demanded in this profession?   Yes _X_   No ____

B. Could you master the fundamental skills without unnecessary difficulty?   Yes _X_   No ____

C. Do you consider the advantageous features indeed advantageous?   Yes _X_   No ____

D. Are the questionable features tolerable?   Yes _X_   No ____

E. Are you willing to meet or exceed the entry-level educational requirements?   Yes ____   No _X_

F. Is earning a lucrative salary the chief or sole reason you want to enter this career?   Yes ____   No _X_

If you answered Yes to F, you can eliminate this career choice. Financial recompense, although pleasant, leaves much in doubt. Career compatibility based on money alone is unstable.

If you answered No to A, B, C, or E, qualify your response with an explanation.

If you answered No to D, isolate the intolerable feature and again explain why.

Sports Psychologist
Career Exploration Rating Sheet

Section —	Points	Comments
interest—very	+4	human behavior is fascinating
career questions	+4	E. hesitate to earn master's

Take the Predicable Personality Type Challenge that corresponds to this career choice. Record your total points and any comments justifying your score.
Total points = 5.

Sports Psychologist
Career Exploration Rating Sheet

Section—	Points	Comments
interest—very	+4	human behavior is fascinating
career questions	+4	E. hesitate to earn master's
personality type	+5	perfect compatibility

Now take your stress temperature. The level of stress a career would impose on you requires your subjective input. Taking your stress temperature is a highly subjective response, requiring quiet introspection. No two people perceive stress the same way. Even with the same person, the same stress may be positive for a while, then switch to negative. You will take your stress temperature using these criteria:

- *Positive stress* is a gentle prod that motivates you to achieve your optimum potential without insult to body or mind.
- *Tolerable stress* is perceived as an invisible force compelling you to accomplish a specific goal. You are consciously aware of the invisible reminder, yet only infrequently do you succumb to psychosomatic illness (physical aches and pains, or depression and anxiety, directly related to inability to cope with stress) as a direct result of stress.
- *Negative stress* stifles your desire to function. You feel overwhelmed by this unseen controlling vibration. The quality of your work decreases, your psychological and physiological well-being are adversely affected, and your concentration diminishes.

Does any aspect of this career choice make you feel uncomfortable? Negative stress could arise from personality incompatibility or from feelings of inability to perform the primary function, master the fundamental skills, or meet educational and licensing requirements.

How do you rate your career stress temperature?

negative = 0
tolerable = +2
positive = +4

A mixture of stress levels is not only possible; it is probable. The type of stress that tends to overpower the remaining two should be your stress temperature. As you already know, a bad mood will reduce your stress temperature.

Add together the points from each section of your Career Exploration Rating Sheet to determine your total.

Total points possible: 18

+4 for interest
+4 for career questions
+5 predictable personality type challenge
+4 stress temperature

17

Sports Psychologist
Career Exploration Rating Sheet

Section—	Points	Comments
interest—very	+4	human behavior is fascinating
career questions	+4	E. hesitate to earn master's
personality type	+5	perfect compatibility
stress temperature	+4	70% positive stress

The Sports Psychologist Career Exploration Rating Sheet received +17 points of a possible +18 points. Medical Exercise Physiologist received +16 points, and Sportswriter earned +17 points. Both Sports Psychologist and

Sportswriter scored +17 points on their Career Exploration Rating Sheets. You *preferred* not to earn a master's degree and take the required state board licensing examination and national certifications for a Sports Psychologist; hence Sportswriter edged out Sports Psychologist.

If you accumulated less than 12 of the 18 points possible, it may be a warning sign that this may not be your best career choice.

Are you pleased with what you have learned about your career choice? If your degree of interest remains very high, and you are still fascinated, you are on the right track. If educational requirements pose a problem, you should consider seeking a career for which you are willing to meet the training requirements without hesitation. If the personality challenge receives less than 50%, or your stress temperature is negative or negligibly tolerable, this may not be a wise career choice for you.

Your three high-scoring careers are your favorite career choices. If you did not have three careers that scored 15 points or more, take stack #2 that was held in reserve and rate those career choices.

SELECT YOUR ALTERNATE CAREER CHOICES

To arrive at your alternate career choices, take your #1 favorite career choice and:

- List two or three of the required or implied fundamental skills in which you excel—written communication, interviewing techniques, meeting deadlines.
- Paraphrase the primary function to correlate with your

fundamental skills—writing about all aspects of sports and the participants.

- Identify two or three predictable personality types that share a mutual compatibility with you and your career choice—independent, self-motivated, studious.
- State the entry-level educational requirements—bachelor's degree.
- What is the salary range?—$16,000 to $30,000 base. Sports-related books and articles could generate additional income.
- Flip through the Career Exploration Fact Sheets and record all the careers with a primary function analogous to your #1 choice—Sports Information Coordinator.

If the primary functions share a commonality, the fundamental skills, educational requirements, and salary range in all probability adhere to the same rule. If in doubt, compare them to your newly discovered alternate career choices.

How many alternate career choices were very similar to your favorite career choice in primary function, fundamental skills, educational requirements, and salary range?—one.

You have one alternate career choice—Sports Information Coordinator. Move on to your #2 favorite career choice, Sports Psychologist, and locate all the choices with analogous primary functions. If necessary, also compare fundamental skills, educational requirements, and salary range. When you have found alternate career choices for each of your favorite career choices, just for fun, try this. Go back to the careers you have rated as slightly or possibly interesting. Are the fundamental skills or predictable personality types compatible with yours? If yes, see if the remainder of the career facts appeal to you enough for you to do a Career Exploration

Rating Sheet. Do not be surprised if you find another career or two you truly like.

References for Review

American Physiological Society, Education Office
9650 Rockville Pike
Bethesda, MD 20014

National Athletic Health Association
575 East Hardy Street
Inglewood, CA 90301

Chronicle Guidance Publications, Inc. (booklets on careers in health and fitness)
Aurora Street Extension
P.O. Box 1190
Moravia, NY 13118-1190

Career World Magazine can be purchased from commercial outlets.

Health Care for the Female Athlete
The Athletics Institute
200 North Castlewood Drive
North Palm Beach, FL 32807

Women's Sports Magazine
310 Town & Country Village
Palo Alto, CA 94301

Women's Sports Foundation
195 Moulton Street
San Francisco, CA 94123

Chapter III

Your Educational Preparation Is the
Foundation of Your Career

SELECT THE TYPE OF EDUCATIONAL PROGRAM BEST SUITED TO YOUR GOALS

Refer to the Career Choice Fact Sheet of your #1 favorite career choice. Look up this data:

- Formal Education and Specialty Training
- Certification and Licensing Regulations (if applicable)
- Universities or Associations

SPORTSWRITER—CAREER EXPLORATION FACT SHEET

Formal Education and Specialty Training:
Bachelor of science in communication arts, journalism, or liberal arts is required. Curriculum should include writing, grammar, humanities, sports, and photography. Sports experience and a sportswriter's internship are valuable.

Certification and Licensing Regulations: Not applicable.

Universities or Associations:
American Council on Education for Journalism
563 Essex Court
Deerfield, IL 60015

By now you should have written to your career choice's association, state licensing board, or a reliable university to ascertain precise educational requirements. If you have investigated more than one career choice, you may have noticed that standards of preparation for some careers are strictly adhered to (the medical field), while others tend to be flexibly structured (aerobics instructor). Your career choice and your personal preference will dictate your course of study.

> Information from the American Council on Education for Journalism confirmed the educational requirements for a sportswriter. The Council suggested three training program options: technical school, university study, or correspondence programs.

Each form of educational preparation offers advantages and, unfortunately, disadvantages. It is your responsibility to sort through the facts and determine the advantages and disadvantages of each, thus selecting the program that will be compatible with your career choice requirements and personal needs.

The six educational programs you will review are:

- conventional university programs
- technical schools
- correspondence programs
- certification workshop/seminars
- company training programs
- —unique—business programs in health and fitness

Universities are schools of higher learning, beyond high school. You attend classes taught by professors on a college campus. Each university independently develops educational programs for the careers taught there. The content of the program may vary from university to university, but the quality remains intact through the university's accreditation by the regulatory agency established to monitor standards. Most universities require an internship period, a supervised work program, before graduation.

Technical schools are like specialty universities and should be accredited. You attend classes taught by professionals in your career choice. Usually the curriculum concentrates almost exclusively on your career choice. Professional expertise is emphasized, and internship is a vital component of the curriculum. Usually, fewer general electives are required for graduation than in a comparable university program. The primary advantage of taking electives is to obtain a broader knowledge base on which to build.

Correspondence programs (home-study programs), once considered substandard to technical schools and universities, have gained acceptance and accreditation. Correspondence programs may be offered by a university or be designed especially to meet the educational requirements of a specific career. It is not unheard of for a correspondence school to require an internship or its equivalent before graduation.

Correspondence School Quality Control

If you question the credibility of any educational program, consult the specialty association of your career to ascertain whether it endorses or accredits the school in question. Consult the state board of education for confirmation. Last, check with your state's Better Business Bureau for guidelines on choosing a reputable educational program.

It is advisable to examine the course material before paying tuition. Short of that, seek a tuition payment plan in which you may lose some money but not much if the program proves unsatisfactory. Check the reputation of any long-distance business *before* sending money.

Avoid any educational program that makes unconditional guarantees of employment after graduation. Ask questions and get the answers before you sign any contract or legal document, or pay any fees.

Certification workshop/seminars combine the principles of university study and correspondence programs. They are intensive, short-term training programs for a specific career. The length of the workshop varies, depending on the career choice, from hours to weeks or months but is generally one to three days. The primary purpose is to drill you on a large quantity of information you are required to know to pass a certification exam.

The certification seminar/workshop process is regulated by independent specialty organizations, not by state or federal laws.

Company training usually implies that you come up through its system. You learn all there is to know about a particular company. But therein lies the danger: You learn only one way—their way. That is fine until you leave that company, but then you may discover that your marketability is restricted without additional education or major revision of habits. However, this can be a plausible training alternative depending on your career choice. Internship is an integral part of this educational program and the company's training program should be accredited by a regulatory agency.

A unique method of training is through *business programs* in health and fitness. A few teaching facilities offer short-

A fitness instructor organizes his free weights.

term, intensive courses (six months or less) in business management in health and fitness. You earn a diploma and could be eligible to complete the requirements for credentials as community college instructor in adult education. For information on such programs, consult your academic adviser or the learning resources center for a listing of college extension programs in health and fitness business management.

Before you write your Educational Program Comparative Chart from the six options discussed, carefully investigate each of them. Reviewing the following illustrations and situations should guide you in the right direction.

Let us suppose your two options are a correspondence program and a university program. Think carefully, and be honest with yourself. Which one would you choose?

Correspondence programs offer a distinct alternative to conventional university study. You fill out the appropriate application forms, pay the tuition fee, and attend classes via your mailbox with auxiliary assistance by telephone as needed. The big question is: Are you and home study compatible? Are you:

- Self-disciplined?
- A self-starter?
- Able to recognize your own weaknesses and develop compensatory mechanisms?
- Able to accept criticism and benefit from it?
- Able to incorporate new information into your lifestyle?
- Serious about doing a good job?
- Able to meet deadlines without reminders?

Next consider *Situation 1:* A friend calls and invites you to a rock concert and a party afterward. The entire gang will be there, live entertainment, and all the frills. You have a difficult assignment that must be postmarked in forty-eight hours. Would you:

- Go with the gang, rationalizing that forty-eight hours is plenty of time to complete an eight-hour assignment? Could you complete the assignment in eight hours?
- Decline the offer, stay home alone, and study?

How would you handle *Situation 2:* Your assignment is exceedingly long, time-consuming, and difficult. You do not really understand the process. Would you:

- Read and reread the material to see if you could independently figure out the process?
- Find the answers in the book and transcribe them onto your worksheet, making a note to study that section before the final exam?
- Call your instructor on the toll-free phone line, get the assistance you need, and then study the section until you understand it?
- Call a friend and ask for help with the assignment?

What are the best responses to the preceding questions? There are none! You must decide from your own perspective which program you would thrive in.

Independent study is more difficult for some people than the conventional classroom, because it lacks an immediate support system (instructor face-to-face and classmates) and pressure to perform.

Write your own comparative chart of correspondence versus university programs; then draw your final conclusion.

COMPARATIVE CHART	
Correspondence Program	University Program
1) Less financial burden after initial course payment	Lodging on campus Transportation to and from Student activity fees
2) Limited social contacts Must actively pursue	Social life automatic
3) Competition—none you can immediately compare to	Envelops you
4) Activities are self-created	Activities are college-created
5) Self-paced	Instructor-paced
6) Relies heavily on written material, videos, and tapes	Access to university facilities Learning resources center Videos, tapes, labs

Now let us add certification workshop/seminars to the university–correspondence school comparison. From the facts presented, which type of program would you select? Write out your comparative chart before arriving at your final conclusion.

COMPARATIVE CHART		
Certification Program	Home Study	University
Location—site changes each time. May have to travel across country or wait for months for one near you (near you may mean a neighboring state).	Same place	Same place
Duration and intensity – short and very intense	Primarily self-imposed	Self- and institution-imposed
Competition extremely intense	Primarily self-imposed	Self- and institution-imposed

Now write out your comparative chart, using the information you obtained from your career choice's specialty association on the educational programs you have chosen. (see Page 94).

Your Educational Program Choice indicates that you will begin with a technical sportswriters' training program to acquire marketable skills. After graduation and profitable employment, you can pursue your bachelor of science in sportswriting.

SELECT A TEACHING INSTITUTION

Now that you have ranked educational programs according to your career choice and personal needs, it is time to

EDUCATIONAL PROGRAM COMPARATIVE CHART

Career Choice	Educational Requirement	Suggested Educational Programs	Virtues	Deficiencies	Fixed Personal Needs	Rank Program Choices
sports-writer	bachelor's (preferred)	technical	intensive experience	few electives	work part-time	1
		university	solid educational foundation	long-time major expense	work experience	2
		correspondence	independent study	no social life		3

examine teaching institutions for that particular type of program.

Consult your academic adviser, state licensing board, specialty association, or learning resources center for a current list of universities, technical schools, certification workshop/seminars, or companies that train for your #1 favorite career choice.

Choose perhaps three to five of the schools, companies, or workshop/seminars that could satisfy your requirements and and send each one a letter asking for information on programs offered, accreditation, and instructors' credentials.

Kathy Kaken
2020 Wishing Well Drive
Quindle, Michigan 48509

Belloak Sportswriters Academy
Office of Admissions
663 Belloak Drive
Belloak, Michigan 48666

Dear Barbara Bennett:

I am interested in attending your technical school. Will you please send me information on prerequisites for entrance, specific graduation requirements for a degree in sportswriting, tuition fees and financial assistance programs, the school's accreditation, and the instructors' credentials.

Your assistance will be greatly appreciated.

Respectfully,

Kathy Kaken

Thoroughly read all the information you receive, and then carefully weigh the positives and negatives of each teaching institution against your objectives.

From the literature, you can extract the facts you need to answer these concerns:

- Outline of the framework of the curriculum on each level: freshman, sophomore, junior, senior.
- What is the program layout? How is it divided: terms, semesters, quarters?
- When and how long are scheduled breaks?

Scrutinize the program's idiosyncrasies. Are there mandatory attendance regulations? If you miss three class sessions, does it mean automatic failure? What penalties are imposed if you withdraw from a class before the term ends, either with a failing mark or a good grade point? If you are dismissed for "excused absence" or "honorable withdrawal," can you retake the class the next term, or must you wait a full school year? If you fail a course, can you retake it? Is there a waiting period before you retake, and must you take other required courses before repeating?

Read the catalogs for facts, not opinions. Do not be lured by false advertising. Be wary of words like "always," "never," or "guaranteed," and of unconditional promises. Be equally suspicious of testimonials by former students that offer a picture and name but not an address. When you can speak directly with students and learn their likes and dislikes of the program and their reasons, the testimony has credibility. Always remember, what may be a repulsive negative to them could be an indispensable asset to you.

To further your research process, answer these questions:

- What advantages does this institution have over its competitors? (Do graduates score higher on certification tests?)
- Is there a waiting list? What is the number of students ahead of you and their grade point average?
- What are the costs?
- What are the prerequisites for entrance?
- What are the graduation requirements?
- Is the program accredited by an educational agency or a specialty association?
- What are the instructors' credentials?

Attempt to interview alumni, current students, and graduates of the institution you are evaluating. Explain the purpose of your interview and ask open-ended, probing questions about their career choice and this teaching institution.
Ask each to explain:

- The virtues and deficiencies of using this teaching institution to prepare for your career choice.
- The opportunities for entry-level employment or advancement as a direct result of this teaching institution.
- The availability of alternate careers, as well as the risks and rewards of a career change as they relate to this teaching institution.
- Any information that could help you finalize your decision on attending this teaching institution.

After you have thanked each for their time and information, sit back for a few moments and meditate. Consider the advice of the professionals you surveyed. Take into account the dates they graduated; college information more than three years old could be obsolete.

Collect and analyze all available information before selecting two or three teaching institutions and writing your personal Teaching Institutions Comparative Chart (see Page 99).

The graduation requirements, accreditation, and instructors' credentials should be analogous. If a teaching institution is lacking in one of the three, eliminate it from your selection and record your reason.

TEACHING INSTITUTIONS COMPARATIVE CHART

Technical Schools	Comparison	Rating
Durdell School of Sportswriters	No accreditations from the state board of academy education nor the Sportswriters Association. Instructors' credentials less than Belloak.	3
Itwell Sportswriters Academy	No accreditation from the state board of academy education. Instructors' credentials less than Belloak.	2
Belloak Sportswriters Academy		1

TEACHING INSTITUTIONS COMPARATIVE CHART

Technical Schools	Belloak Sportswriters Academy	Itwell Sportswriters Academy	Durdell School of Sportswriters
entrance prerequisites	gives own exam	administers SAT	gives own exam
advantages	best academic program	job placement assistance after graduation	close to home
graduation requirements	2.0 GPA internship	2.0 GPA internship	2.0 GPA internship
school accreditation	educational/ association	association only	no accreditation
instructors' credentials	master's degrees experienced sportswriters	majority bachelor's experienced sportswriters	bachelor's and master's degrees experienced sportswriters
costs	$25. per credit hour	comparable	comparable
waiting list	none if GPA 3.2 or above	none	none

If you have alternate forms of educational programs you wish to study, do so at this time.

Career Choice	Educational Requirements	Rank Program Choices	Studied
Sportswriter	Bachelor's (preferred)	Technical	Yes
		University	No
		Correspondence	No

Make your choice from the educational programs you have analyzed and summarize the prerequisite requirements. As your record now stands, can you meet or exceed the requirements? If so, excellent! Do not take your academic standing for granted. The competition can be merciless. If you do not meet the requirements, now is your golden opportunity to make the changes that will mold your future to your specifications.

Remember, while you are still in high school is the time to determine your career choice educational requirements and make the necessary preparations. Any prerequisite courses not taken in high school will most certainly be required once you are admitted to the teaching institution. Some teaching institutions place students on probationary status until the prerequisites are met.

If you cannot meet the required educational standards, make a list of the courses you need and discuss your predicament with your academic adviser. Begin to incorporate these classes into your curriculum, starting with those that are most important. Perhaps a journalism class would precede a history elective if your goal is to be a sportswriter. If college is in your plans, college preparatory courses provide an excellent foundation. Your grade point average can be your friend or foe. A high percentage of teaching institutions check high school averages. If your grade point is substandard, make an extra effort to raise it above the minimum required for admission to the teaching institution you have selected. Pave your smooth transition from high school to college by recognizing and exceeding standards *before* they become requirements.

Hints Worth Remembering

- Before you register at your chosen teaching institution, if possible, visit the institution to get a feel for the atmosphere and philosophy. If it is a correspondence program or a certification workshop/seminar, make a telephone call and converse with some of the personnel. Perhaps you can schedule a telephone interview with the program director or one of the instructors of the program you wish to pursue.
- If you are seriously interested in attending a nonaccredited educational program, it is worth your time to research why it is not accredited. It is best to attend an accredited program when possible.
- If your funds are short, apply for financial aid well in advance.
- An alternative, if you are short on cash or lack the scholastic aptitude for a four-year university degree, is to attend a junior college, raise your grade point, and bank the dollars you save in tuition fees.
- Take a second look at your current career choice.

    —What do you want your career status to be in five years; in ten years?

—Are you an ambitious workaholic scaling the corporate ladder, or an aspiring entrepreneur?

—How much time, money, and energy are you willing to invest in your career endeavor?

—Does your favorite career choice have educational requirements similar to those of your alternate choices? If the field of sportswriting became saturated, and your alternate choice was sports information coordinator, what additional training would be needed to make the career change?

Why place such emphasis on the distant future? The way you prepare yourself today will be the controlling element of your tomorrows. In our ever-changing society many unsuspecting people have been displaced. Once displaced, you may need comprehensive retraining in a new career before reentering the job market. Unplanned career changes can be disruptive. Be alert to possible pitfalls and take steps to avoid them or to make the career switch as effortless as possible.

WALK THROUGH THE ADMISSION PROCEDURE

Your next step is to gain admission into the educational program of your choice.

The general admission procedures of universities and technical schools are similar. Usually the first step is to procure an application for admission. Submit the completed application form, an official copy of your high school transcripts, your ACT (American College Test) or SAT (Scholastic Aptitude Test) results, any other forms required. The vast majority of colleges recommend that high school students submit completed paperwork about one year before planned admission. Early in your senior year is best.

After acceptance to the university, you register at a prescribed time. You then meet with your academic adviser, select suitable classes, receive your student ID (identification) card, review your financial status, make housing arrangements, reserve your textbooks, tour the campus, and learn the particularities of the school. If you are to live on campus, you will be expected to move into the residence hall at a given time. Most universities offer get-acquainted programs for freshmen, before classes begin as well as after.

The following might be your general requirements checklist for college admission:

- Complete your application and submit it, along with transcripts and SAT or ACT results, by October of your senior year. The admissions office will verify your acceptance, usually by letter. You may receive your student ID number at this time. It would behoove you to memorize that number; it is your new name.
- Sometimes you must supply written references. Some schools require a personal interview.
- If you are going to live on campus, arrange for your housing early. Finish and submit the paperwork before the specified deadline.
- Consult with your academic adviser. Openly and realistically communicate your needs, concerns, goals, strengths, and weaknesses. The purpose of this meeting is to develop an individualized program to satisfy your specific needs.
- If your budget is tight, check out the financial assistance programs offered through the university. Inquire early for financial aid. If for any reason it is denied, alternate

arrangements can still be made before classes commence.

- Registering for classes can be a tedious chore, especially if your approach is disorganized and incomplete. Before you register, find out exactly what data are needed and prepare the paperwork well in advance. Wear comfortable clothing and shoes. Do not forget essentials like your driver's license and social security number.
- After registration is finalized, you report to the dormitory or classes as scheduled. Your campus life has begun!

Admission to correspondence programs and certification workshop/seminars can usually be done by mail.

PREPARE YOUR FINANCIAL STATEMENT

Calculate your budget by assessing your financial resources and calculating your projected expenses. Then total your fees, including entrance and class fees, lab fees, and one-time-only student activity fees. What living arrangements are you making? Is the school commutable from home? Will you live in a dorm? Does the cost of the dorm include food? What are the parking arrangements? Must you pay for the parking permit in a lump sum, or can you use the installment plan? Count the fringes, too. Will you have a phone bill to contend with? If you are long-winded, that could be a deficit. What is your budgeted weekly allowance for nonessentials? Do you have the financial resources to meet your needs, or should you seek assistance? Using this information, write your financial statement.

Personal Financial Resources		Expenses Fall Term	
Savings account	$3,000	Tuition	
Part-time		(12 credits)	$2,400
employment	2,500	Fees and	
Other resources	_____	textbooks	310
		Room and board	3,200
Total projected		Parking	125
income	$5,500	Phone	120
		Nonessentials	800
		Clothing	500
			$7,555

Recognizing that you lack the necessary funds to attend one term, you next evaluate the financial assistance programs available to you.

Financial assistance programs provide funds for students to pay for educational expenses. Although there are distinct differences, the major points are universal. All financial assistance programs should be applied for well in advance. Program eligibility requirements may be stringent.

What type of aid does your school offer: work-study, grants, loans? If you are contemplating a student loan, is there a ceiling? What are the terms of repayment and the interest rate? What are the eligibility requirements? Does the school issue or honor grants? Who is eligible for a grant? Are there grounds on which it must be repaid? Are scholarships issued? What are the eligibility requirements? Who grants scholarships? Are there scholastic achievement stipulations? What work-study programs are offered through the school?

Financial assistance programs fall into four primary groups: loans, grants, scholarships, and work-study programs. Each category has a multitude of subdivisions. Seek knowledgeable assistance if you need help in deciphering them. Thoroughly investigate all the alternatives before making your selection.

Scholarships can differ greatly from one institution to another. They are awarded to qualified students by the school or by a professional organization. Some community organizations sponsor a health and fitness student, or the Department of Education may provide funding. Usually, scholarship recipients must demonstrate financial need and scholastic achievement. Scholarships do not have to be repaid.

Loans are of two principal types. The first is the guaranteed student loan, which is made by a bank, a credit union, or a savings and loan association, and is backed by the goverment. It has a low interest rate. The second type, the National Direct Student Loan, is more difficult to obtain. This, too, is at a low interest rate and is approved and granted through the institution. Recipients must demonstrate financial hardship. If you are having difficulty finding a lender, your state guarantee program is your best source of information on student loans.

Grants are federally funded monies awarded to eligible recipients based on several factors, including financial need. The Pell Grant Program (basic educational opportunity grant) is the most common. Grants do not have to be repaid.

Work-study programs are provided by the institution to help with financial obligations. They offer part-time (20 hours or less per week) on-campus employment. If the on-campus opportunities are limited or unsatisfactory, most campuses list off-campus employment prospects.

Recently a new financial assistance package was established, the ConSern Student Loan Program. For further information call 202-265-1313. A new corporation, University Support Services, issues the loans. Students may borrow $1,500 to 15,000 annually, to a cumulative amount of $60,000, which may be paid back over a 12-year period. Eligibility is determined by creditworthiness, not family income.

The following sources can help you in obtaining financial assistance:

The American Medical Association provides information on how to finance a medical career.

The American Medical Association
535 Dearborn Street
Chicago, IL 60610

The Women's Sports Foundation annually publishes a scholarship guide aimed at women in health and fitness careers. Send $1.00 for postage and handling fees to:

Women's Sports Foundation
195 Moulton Street
San Francisco, CA 94123

For additional information, write to:
National Collegiate Athletic Association
P.O. Box 1906
Mission, KS 66201

References for Review

Teaching Facilities and Certification Programs

International Correspondence Schools
925 Oak Street
Scranton, PA 18508-9989

American College of Sports Medicine
P.O. Box 1440
Indianapolis, IN 46206

Aerobics and Fitness Association of America
15250 Ventura Boulevard
Sherman Oaks, CA 91403

International Dance-Exercise Association and Foundation
4501 Mission Bay Drive
San Diego, CA 92109

Chapter IV

The Health and Fitness Career Lifeline

STATE YOUR CAREER GOALS

- What is your immediate career goal?
- What are your current obligations that cannot be changed?
- What personal needs are you unwilling to alter?
- Are your personal and career goals compatible? If not, identify the conflicts.
  - If there are conflicts between your personal and career goals, are you willing to make the alterations that would facilitate a harmonious balance?
  - If you are unwilling to make such adjustments, you may find it advantageous to revise your career goals.

IDENTIFY JOB-FINDING SOURCES

You have devoted valuable time, money, and energy to achieving your career status in health and fitness. It is of paramount importance for you to scrutinize job leads from these sources: conventional, unconventional, and specialty organizations.

Three of the most common *conventional* methods of job-hunting are the yellow pages of the telephone book,

Career Goal	Personal Needs	Conflicts/ Compatible	Satisfactory Adjustment
Immediate Obtain full-time employment as sportswriter	Member of Sportswriters Association	Compatible	
	Work part-time	Conflict with class time	Talk with supervisor; change hours
	Weekend trips with friends	Conflict; Academy out of town	Must miss some trips

newspaper classified advertisements, and networking with colleagues. All generate referrals. However, the quality and source of a job lead should be carefully examined before you follow through. What criteria would you use to determine which are and which are not solid leads?

- Is there a contact person or department?
- Are the prospective candidate's qualifications listed?
- Is there a brief job description?
- Is an address or phone number given?
- Is a preferred method of application indicated?

Perhaps you have two job leads. The first is an advertisement you read in your specialty organization's newsletter:

SPORTSWRITER

Opportunity exists for an energetic, independent journalist for full time. Qualified candidate must possess BA in Journalism, with one year's experience preferred. Competitive wage and excellent benefit package. Qualified individuals may submit résumé to:
Sport Ball
300 Strike Drive
Ballvale, Michigan 48666
R. Spelvel, President

The second lead you received from a colleague you met for the first time at a sportswriters' workshop-seminar. The Belloak *News*, of Belloak, Michigan, has a vacancy for a sportswriter.

Is essential information missing from the first job lead? If you said "no", you are correct.

What facts are missing from the second job lead? Contact person, exact location (address or telephone number), and qualifications are three key elements.

Which would you pursue first? Number one, because you have all the required information. Either or both vacancies could be filled by the time you collected the facts for number two and then sent your cover letter and résumé.

The advantages of conventional job-finding sources are availability and familiarity. The disadvantages are that they are confined to a given geographical location, and that job offers in unique or specialty areas are often omitted.

Unconventional job-finding sources may open more doors to employment than the conventional means. Unfortunately, some people are unaware that they exist or do not realize their full potential. Before you read the want ads or dial the phone, you may want to explore some of these alternatives.

Your county service department may have a listing of health and fitness services employment opportunities for your area. The library may have reference books in which you can find employment ideas. Some educational programs offer placement services for their graduates and for qualified graduates of other programs. Indispensable job information can be found in general health and fitness magazines and by attending meetings of your specialty association.

The advantages of unconventional job-finding sources are essentially two: They broaden the possibilities offered by conventional means, and as a direct result they hold the potential for increased financial rewards.

Among disadvantages, exhaustive research may be required to reveal a prospective employer. A direct or indirect fee may be charged by some sources. Direct fees are charged for placement services by an organization. Indirect charges are incurred when you join a specialty organization and must pay membership dues.

Specialty job-finding sources are designed to help professionals in health and fitness fields locate a company that needs their particular expertise. Virtually every division of health and fitness has an association from which members can obtain statistics and idiosyncrasies regarding employment in its specialty. Other specialty job-finding sources include newsletters and placement agencies.

The primary advantages of specialty job-finding sources are unrestricted geographical listings and an abundance of inside information on employment possibilities. They are very time-efficient, in that your preliminary market research has been done for you by a reliable source.

Among the disadvantages, specialty job-finding sources are an asset only to a specialist in that career. Also, travel expenses to conduct your presearch might be prohibitive, or organization membership dues could be a deterrent.

How and when would you utilize each of the three sources to procure job leads?

- Ask the Sportswriters Association for its newsletter and other publications that carry job leads.
- Aggressively evaluate the unconventional sources whenever possible.
- Conventional sources require ongoing periodic review (Sunday advertisements).

You expect that the Sportswriters Association will be your best source of leads but will examine all sources.

Women jobseekers may want to investigate:

Wider Opportunities for Women
1511 K Street, NW
Washington, DC 20005

Your county may have a Women's Resource Center to offer additional leads.

SEEK THE POSITION YOU WANT

Where should you begin? Your self-marketing package consisting of your résumé, cover letter, and other vital components must convince the prospective employer that you are the best candidate for this position. Before you can begin, ideally you need to know three factors:

- Your precise qualifications, personality type, and limitations (you could conceivably be asked how you compensate for your limitations.
- The company's precise needs and expectations.
- The competition's precise qualifications, personality type, limitations, and compensatory mechanisms.

In fact, the competition's status is known only to the prospective company. You must maneuver around that blind spot by:

- Comprehensive, serious self-study to present your best professional image.
- Research of every detail about the prospective company.

To gather the data you need, commence with your career and personal assessment.

- What is your career goal?
  —Sportswriter.
- Do you have geographical location restrictions? If yes, be specific in listing them.
  —Michigan, lower peninsula.
- How soon before you must be gainfully employed? Translated, how long can you take to find the job you want?
  —Six months maximum.
- What type of setting appeals to you?
  —First choice, rural; second, small town; no city.
- What is your preference for a work environment: busy and corporately structured, or quiet and flexible?
  —Quiet and flexible.
- Total your basic living expenses for one year. Next, calculate your salary requirements to meet your cost of living. Try to anticipate special expenses over the next year (you may need a new car), and add them to your list. Is your salary range still adequate?
  —Basic Living Expenses: $18,000, salary range adequate.

- Identify your personal needs.
  —You are unable to travel overnight.
- What personal attitudes, habits, standards, and philosophies would be major factors in determining job prospects?
  —Condescending attitude by superiors toward subordinates will not be tolerated.
  —Violation of legal, moral, or ethical values will not be tolerated.
  —Overt philosophies that stifle an employee's work performance will not be tolerated.

Assemble and organize the data from your career and personal assessment which you will incorporate into securing the position you want. Use the three job-finding sources to locate ten to twenty prospective employers that could accommodate your career and personal needs.

Company Name	Job-Finding Source
Belloak *County Line*	Newspaper advertisement
Belloak *News*	Conventional–networking
Decurves Spots Sport	Specialty magazine advertisement
Sports Ball	Specialty magazine advertisement

Send a brief letter to each prospective employer on your list, requesting business literature.

Kathy Kaken
2020 Wishing Well Drive
Quindle, Michigan 48509

Sports Ball
Public Relations Department:
300 Strike Drive
Ballvale, Michigan 48666

Gentlemen:

Please send me any literature you have available describing your compnay's product (or service). Your assistance is greatly appreciated.

Respectfully,

Kathy Kaken

The sole purpose of this letter is to gather information. It is premature to mention that you are seeking employment until you know whether you can meet this company's expectations and the company can satisfy your needs, and until you have completed your preliminary screening of each company on your list.

The business literature you receive from the companies on your list should provide you with a basis for obtaining answers to other important questions.

- Read each piece of business literature critically, and eliminate those companies that do not meet your personal or career criteria.
- Rank the remaining prospective employers in order of compatibility and preference.

Transcribe the data from your career and personal assessment and the prospective employers' literature to Prospective Employer Cards. You might use a steno notebook, 5″ x 7″ index cards, or a junior legal pad for a quick, one-stop reference check for all your prospective employers' information.

Prospective Employer Card
Self-Marketing Notes (S.M.N.)

Prospective Employer   Rated #1
Name
Address
Contact Person and Title
Phone #

S.M.N.
  Excellent geographical location
  Salary and perks are respectable
  Setting: rural
  Environment: apparently quiet
  Computerized technology for sportswriter

Front of 5″ x7″ Index Card

Presearch Data (recorded during your presearch visit)	Employer:
	Date Initiated:
Observations:	Method of Contact: (phone, mail, personal)
Communication:	Date Void:
Conclusions:	Comments:

Back of 5″ x 7″ Index Card

Next, establish how you will approach your job-hunting project. Will you type your own cover letters and résumé, or have them done by a word processor? What hours will you be available to answer your phone? Will someone answer your phone in your absence, or will you use a telephone answering device to record messages? Remember, a missed call could mean a lost job opportunity.

Record all your expenses as they occur; they may be tax-deductible. Another thought, your prospective employer may give you complete or partial reimbursement if you are hired. Keep an expense record for each prospective employer.

Expense Record
Expense record for _____
company name

Travel (gas, food)   Clothes (if requirement of
                                                  employment)

Phone (bill, answering   Miscellaneous
  service)
Job Package (detailed
  explanation later)

Presearch your prospective employers. This phase is critical to success in obtaining the position best suited to your career and personal convictions. A judicious performance will yield the exact job you want. A superficial scanning may result in unnecessary failure. Planning and evaluating are your tools to success.

Flip through your Prospective Employer Cards; refresh

your memory on your self-marketing notes and the literature received from each prospective employer. Your top five choices will constitute your initial presearch investigation. File the remainder of your Prospective Employer Cards; do not discard.

Before you start your intensive presearch study, do a preliminary quick-scan to determine if a prospective employer is worth the time investment required. This is the fun part!

Your quick-scan presearch consists of basic on-site observations and analysis of the prospective employer. Jump in your car, or on the bus or subway, and make a practice run to the prospective employer. Plan to travel during peak rush-hour traffic. Is this a relaxing trip, or are you aboard the white-knuckle express? One-way streets, traffic jams, and overcrowded trains all contribute to negative stress and can exhaust you before you commence your workday. Are these small considerations? Maybe, but they could be the determining factor.

Once on location, capitalize on your observational skills. Is the visitors' parking lot well-kept or littered? Is there a parking attendant? Are the lawn and shrubs well manicured or neglected?

Why are these and similar observations significant? They give you an overview of the management's basic philosophies and the employees' attitudes and work habits. If these standards meet your approval, relax and continue your quick-scan. If the circumstances are unsatisfactory, waste no time; leave and continue to your next prospective employer. Make notes on your Prospective Employer Card of the conditions you found deplorable or your specific reasons for disapproval.

If this prospective employer is still a viable candidate,

Telemarketing is an important aspect of public relations.

observe the visitors' and employees' behavioral transactions. Do company comployees and clients interact with one another, or do they refrain from communicating? Specifically observe the employees. Do most of them send vibrations of contentment with pleasant facial expressions, or are most of them sober, looking angry or depressed? Are negative or positive reactions prevalent? Are the employees approachable? As you make your subjective judgment, however, look carefully at the total picture. Everyone can experience a bad day, and one incident can have traumatic effects on all staff.

Now observe the employees' appearance. Are the majority neat and clean, or wrinkled and dirty? Are you impressed with your findings? If no, jot down major reasons for discontent and exit promptly. If yes, make a few pertinent notes and plan for a return presearch trip. Record your travel time during rush hour, parking costs for an employee, route directions to the site, and special facts to remember. Before you leave, make detailed notes on visitors' attire.

If equipment is used, does it seem to be well maintained, functional, and current? Or is it functionally defective or antiquated?

Do you still like what you see? As you continue your quick-scan, check the employees' parking lot and notice the layout. Does the lighting seem adequate for after dark? Is it close to the employee exit door? It may be worthwhile to check safety features such as security guards on duty or escorts available.

When you arrive home, while details are still fresh in your mind, plan your presearch investigation for the next day, if possible. Plan your wardrobe and accessories, approximating the dress of the visitors on your quick-scan visit so that you will blend in and become one of the crowd. Your presearch is not an advertised appearance. You are conducting an unobtrusive fact-finding mission to decide whether you would like to work there. Update your Prospective Employer Card in preparation for tomorrow.

For now, your presearch arrival time has to be during peak business hours, to permit you to flow with the clients. Ideally, it should be during the hours you want to work. It is advisable to arrive half an hour before your work would commence, enabling you to encounter as many information-givers as possible. Observe and evaluate the prospective employer's personnel as a unit, noticing attitudes, department affiliations, personal habits, and communication skills.

Upon arrival, walk to the main entrance of the building, naturally, slowly, and deliberately. Absorb all the data your senses provide. Your demeanor should be free, relaxed, and friendly. How do the employees react to you? Are they responsive to one another? Once in the lobby, head for the rest room and freshen up. As you leave the rest room, take the opportunity to observe the atmosphere. Is it just busy, or very confused? Are the employees helpful, or aloof? Do most of them seem happy, or discontented? Is the general atmosphere flighty or organized, noisy or quiet? Next, study the physical layout. Where would you be working? A small, partitioned cubbyhole, or a spacious, attractively designed office? Read and absorb all posted information. Do the rules seem flexible, or rigid? Are the rules strictly adhered to, or only quasi-enforced? Who has been honored for contributions, and what kind? Have employees received awards for outstanding achievements or length of service? Or is attention focused on the unknown who made a large financial donation? Note the prospective employer's priorities. Are employees' rights (nonsmokers) posted and taken seriously? What governing agencies accredit this company? What do you see: disorganization, uniformity, too stuffy, too large, too small, challenging, boring? Are you impressed or depressed? If it does not meet your specifications, conserve your energy, make notes, and return home.

If you are interested, stick around! There is more to do. Activate your communication skills as you continue your presearch investigation. Inconspicuously listen to the content and tone of conversations between employees and clients and among employees. Do clients seem pleased or disgruntled with the service they have received or the product purchased? Can you isolate a reason? Is one employee being blamed? Is it an unjustified complaint of a trivial nature, or a legitimate gripe? Attempt to isolate the cause of dissatisfaction. If several clients voice the same negative opinion, you could consider the circumstances and investigate further. However, your wisest choice is probably to leave promptly and proceed with a new candidate from your Prospective Employer list. Most internal company problems are difficult to diagnose and resolve.

If circumstances still meet your specifications, try to find a friendly employee whom you can engage in conversation. Introduce yourself, explain the reason for your visit, say that you are impressed, and ask an open-ended question. Is this place as pleasant to work in as it seems? If you are fortunate, this employee will be forthcoming. If not, do not press. Just say thank you and disappear. Then enter comments on your Prospective Employer Card, consider your visit a victory, and head home. You may find it advantageous to visit this prospective employer two or three times, to confirm that there are no conflicts in your observations.

Repeat this process with each prospective employer until you have collected all the facts you need to make an intelligent decision. Once you have narrowed your choices down to two or three, you are ready to write your health and fitness career job-winning package.

COMPOSE YOUR JOB-WINNING PACKAGE

Write your résumé, cover letter, and components slanted to the employer of your choice. The Four C's to remember are: mail your résumé and cover letter to the *correct* person, containing the *correct* message, in the *correct* format, at the *correct* time.

Referring to your Prospective Employer File Card, address your mailing to the contact person stated. That is the correct person. If a contact person is missing, check the job-finding source that provided this employer and the literature you received from the company. If you still lack a contact person, call the organization and ask for the name of the Editor-in-Chief of Sports. It is imperative that your employment package reach the Sports Department supervisor.

The correct message must be compatible with the company's philosophies and with your personal and professional assessment. Combine the philosophies you discovered in your presearch investigation and your assessment of the company. Tell the company how your skills complement its needs and expectations.

The correct format is the proper presentation of your résumé and cover letter.

The correct time to apply for a position coincides with the employer's need to fill a position. Naturally, the optimum time to apply for work immediately precedes the need. This is where your professional networking is an invaluable assessment tool. Lacking networking insights, check your presearch survey. You may have picked up clues to internal factors that create specific needs. Consider vacation shortages, especially summertime. During holidays and weekends, staffing is at a minimum. You may want to consider contingency or call-in relief status, especially if part-time work is your preference. If you wish contingency status, or do not mind irregular hours, be sure to mention it in your cover letter. It is a definite selling point. Keep in mind that the more flexible you are, the more in demand you will be. Volunteering for out-of-town assignments could make you a valuable asset.

Your Job-winning Package is a written fact sheet of your achievements, personality characteristics, career goals, natural abilities, and work-related habits. When presented as a complete unit, your written image becomes visible to the reader. The psychological, emotional, and mental you comes to life. Therefore, it is critical to your success that you choose and use action words that present you in the most favorable light.

What comprises your Job-winning Package? Your résumé and cover letter that convey your central theme, your achievement record, your career goals, and your continuing education summary.

- State your career goals now and in the future, and possible strategies to meet those goals. Pull this data from your reference sheets.
- Use your superior achievements sheet to describe an exceptional accomplishment, such as having made a major contribution that would enhance your career potential.
- Your continuing education sheet lists the courses you

have taken that exceed minimum requirements for your favorite career choice. It can also mention training programs or extracurricular community activities you have engaged in that facilitated health and fitness-oriented learning. Specialty journals or textbooks you have read on your own may or may not be granted official credit.

- List any professional affiliation such as membership in professional organizations, clubs, and associations that foster professional growth.

- Your cover letter offers your prospective employer the first glimpse of your written image. If compatibility has been established with the employer, and you have properly handled your cover letter, your candidacy will probably be considered. If improperly handled, even though you have the qualifications, you could lose all chances of getting the job you want.

- Your résumé should tell the employer where you have worked and your accomplishments during your tenure. If you are a recent graduate, you should give your school and your anticipated date of graduation, as well as noteworthy academic accomplishments.

- A cover letter–résumé is a condensed and combined version of the cover letter and résumé. It is ideally used by one with a fragile employment history, or by new graduates.

- Your letters of reference are evidence of your achievements and attributes. Each is a valuable testimony of your excellence. Who is qualified to write your letters of reference? A previous employer, an instructor, or a professional in your field. Character references can be from anyone who is not a relative, preferably a reputable professional in your career choice, or a respected community leader. To assure yourself of getting a letter of reference, you should request it before your work relationship terminates and your status becomes history. After graduation, an instructor may forget some of your outstanding features. A letter of reference is written by someone who admires you and wants to help you achieve your career and personal aspirations. Do not misuse letters of reference. Always request permission from the writers before submitting letters. If possible, inform them who might be calling or writing, and when.

You will elaborate on your *career goals*. List in order of importance two to three of the goals you would expect to achieve as an entry-level employee during the next 12 months.

- Editor and sportswriter for a specialty sports magazine.
- Write my own sports column for a major metropolitan newspaper.
- Complete sports coverage for a small-town newspaper.

Research each goal to determine for which you have the educational and technical training, and which would need additional training and education to pursue. Elementary prerequisites for these positions are as follows:

- Complete sports coverage for a small-town newspaper: Technical school graduate with sports knowledge and experience.
- Sports column in major metropolitan newspaper:

Minimum of bachelor's degree in journalism with specialty training in sports; sports knowledge and two to three years' field experience as a sportswriter.

● Editor and sportswriter for a specialty sports magazine: Bachelor's in journalism with three to five years' field experience; sports knowledge required.

Eliminate those that do not meet your immediate time frame.

● Major metropolitan newspaper.
● Specialty sports magazine.

Write the final copy of your career goals.

● To secure employment as a sportswriter for a local newspaper, where my technical training, in-depth sports knowledge, and experience will be used to mutual benefit, providing financial rewards compatible with my responsibilities, and offering possibilities of advancement.

Your *superior achievements sheet* tells your prospective employer about a career-related, unique, or profound accomplishment, or an unusual sportswriting talent you possess. The final copy of your superior achievements sheet may read like this:

● You attended a class A baseball game out of state when a local talent was scouted and signed by a major league team. You interviewed the team manager and the local talent and wrote the story, which was published in the sports section of your local paper.

Your *continuing education sheet* includes all learning experiences that enhance your writing talents or broaden your sportswriter's knowledge base.

Continuing education is defined as a lifelong learning process. It can mean formal education, for which you receive college credit; or informal learning, which can be company-sponsored training workshop/seminars.

Record all your continuing education during the last five years:

- "No Nonsense Sports Journalism"
  Journalist Specialty
  April/May 90   (magazine)
  5/90   .3 CEU

- "The Talking Pen"
  seminar/workshop
  6/90   2 credits
  Belloak, Michigan   48666

If you have more than one page, eliminate the oldest or least significant first, with magazine articles being least creditable. If you are a new graduate, highlight all extra career-related projects in which you have been involved.

Place your continuing education in chronological order, with the most recent first. If you have only a few as a new graduate, place the emphasis on the most significant.

Your *professional affiliations* should be listed on a separate sheet of paper. (If you have not joined an association specializing in your career choice, you may want to investigate the possibility. Specialty associations offer numerous benefits, answer many of your questions, offer networking, and give you a head start.)

Your *cover letter* should help the prospective employer decide whether to take the time to read your résumé. It reveals such traits as self-confidence, ability to communicate, accuracy when recording facts, stability, and integrity. If you are logical, organized, and neat, the depth of your people skills will also be revealed. It is amazing what a few sentences can tell an insightful reader. *Note*: A cover letter is one page maximum; state your facts clearly and concisely.

- Contents and flow of your cover letter should state your reason for writing.
- Introduce the prospective employer to your résumé and job-winning package.
- Let your qualifications state why you are the ideal candidate for the position. (Be certain to specify what position you are applying for; the organization may have more than one vacancy to fill.)
- Highlight your special achievements and ways you could benefit this particular company.
- Briefly mention your primary career goal.
- State your interview follow-up plan.

Kathy Kaken
2020 Wishing Well Drive
Quindle, Michigan 48509
1-111-888-2525

Mr. Allen Calstrike
Editorial Director
I.C. Sportsview
6900 Bell River Drive
Belloak, Michigan 48666

Dear Mr. Calstrike:
    In response to your advertisement in the Belloak

County Line, I am enclosing my résumé. I am interested in a sportswriter position.

I am a recent graduate of Belloak Sportswriters Academy.

I am available for immediate assignment. Overnight travel is a welcome change of pace. I cope effectively with stress, and I am able to meet deadlines.

I attended a class A baseball game out of state when a local talent was scouted and signed by a major league team. I interviewed the team manager and the local talent and wrote the story, which was published in the sports section of our local paper.

My immediate goal is to establish rapport with other employees. I would like to emphasize my skills in baseball, basketball, and track and field coverage. I was captain of my high school varsity volleyball team for three years. I have studied sports and have an in-depth knowledge of procedures, rules, and strategies in most sports.

I will be available for an interview from February 10 through 21. Acknowledgment of receipt of the enclosed résumé would be greatly appreciated. For your convenience, a self-addressed stamped envelope has been provided for that purpose. Thank you for your time and consideration.

Respectfully,

Kathy Kaken

The contents of your résumé or cover letter-résumé would be arrived at the same way.

If you are a student or recent graduate without an

impressive employment record, take two sheets of paper and mark one classroom theory and one field practicum. List your achievements in each area that are consistent with your career goals.

Classroom Theory

Studied the details of writing attention-grabbing sports coverage.
Demonstrated seven mock scenes.
Wrote strategies for winning tennis.

Field Practicum

Editor of the Belloak Sportswriters Academy's *Gazette*.
Attended a class A baseball game out of state when a local talent was scouted and signed by a major league team. Interviewed the team manager and the local talent, and wrote the story, which was published in the sports section of our local paper.

Skills	Accomplishments

- Wrote strategies for winning tennis.
- Demonstrated seven mock scenes.
- Studied writing attention-grabbing sports coverage.
- Editor of the Belloak Sportswriters Academy's *Gazette*.
- Attended a class A baseball game out of state when a local talent was scouted and signed by

> a major league team. Interviewed the team
> manager and the local talent and wrote the
> story, which was published in the sports
> section of our local paper.

Set up two columns headed Skills and Accomplishments.
Transfer all your accomplishments to this sheet.
Identify the skills that made your accomplishments
possible.

Skills	Accomplishments

Communication
Motivation
Organization
Self-starter
Use of resources
Prioritizing
Retain and apply
   learned data
Interpersonal
  skills
	• Wrote strategies for winning tennis.
	• Demonstrated seven mock scenes.
	• Studied writing attention-grabbing sports coverage.
	• Editor of the Belloak Sportswriters Academy's *Gazette*.
	• Attended a class A baseball game out of state when a local talent was scouted and signed by a major league team. Interviewed the team manager and the local talent and wrote the story, which was published in the sports section of our local paper.

Number the skills and match them to the corresponding
accomplishments. It may require several skills to make one
accomplishment.

Skills	Accomplishments	Match

1-Communication
2-Motivation
3-Organization
4-Self-starter
5-Use of
  resources
6-Prioritizing
7-Retain and
  apply learned
  data
8-Interpersonal
  skills
	• Attended a class A
	baseball game out of
	state when a local talent
	was scouted and signed
	by a major league team.
	Interviewed the team
	manager and the local
	talent and wrote the
	story, which was
	published in the sports
	section of our local
	paper.
		1, 2
		3, 4
		5, 6
		7, 8

You will want to make a Résumé Content Chart. List your achievements and analyze each (see Page 135).

This is not a difficult exercise. However, some people omit important sections, because they do not see how what they do can have such a tremendous impact on their environment and other people. Think *self-worth* as you complete this section.

Now that you have collected all the information required to write your résumé, here are a few common-sense rules. Résumés are best kept to one page, but two pages is the absolute maximum. Most employers do not have time to read page after page; besides, too much information distracts from your outstanding qualities.

As shown in the following paragraph, the body of your résumé will be derived from your Résumé Content Chart, which you have just completed.

RÉSUMÉ CONTENT CHART

1 Accomplishment	2 Who Was Affected	3 Results	4 Skills Required	5 Who Commended Your Contribution
1) Sports feature published in local newspaper	Local talent Community Self Manager	Positive publicity for local talent, community, self, manager, team Award for the sports feature	Communication Motivation Organization Self-starter Use of resources Prioritizing Retain and apply learned data Interpersonal skills	Newspaper editor Community Local talent Sports Mind Writers' Association

Discovered a local talent's news-breaking sports story. Pursued an on-site account of the manager of a professional team signing a local talent. Composed a sports feature and submitted it to our local paper. The benefactors of the newspaper article were the local talent, the community, the team and its manager, and writer. Sports feature received commendations from the newspaper editor, community, and local talent.

Now construct the final copy of your rèsumè.

Career Goal:

To secure employment as a sportswriter for a local newspaper, where my technical training, in-depth sports knowledge, and sports experience will be used to mutual benefit, providing financial rewards compatible with my responsibilities, and offering possibilities of advancement.

Formal Education:

Belloak Sportswriters Academy
Belloak, Michigan   48666

Brief Job Description:

Graduated 6/16/90 with a diploma in sportswriting and a grade point average of 3.65. Studied the details of writing attention-grabbing sports coverage.

Major Accomplishments:

Sports Mind Writers' Association award for the sports feature on a local talent.
Wrote strategies for winning tennis.

Continuing Education Credentials:

"The Talking Pen"
seminar/workshop

6/90   2 credits
Belloak, Michigan   48666

"No Nonsense Sports Journalism"
Journalist Specialty
April/May 90   (magazine)
5/90   .3 CEU

Professional Affiliations:
Sportswriters Golden Rule
268 Spiral Drive
Springboard, South Dakota   79790

Other Data:
Salary open to negotiation.
References available upon request.

Following are suggested contents of a letter of reference written by another for you.

- If written by an employer, it should give dates of employment. If written by an instructor, a counselor, a community leader, a pastor, or a coach, give the length of acquaintanceship.
- Outline your major accomplishments.
- State your health and attendance record.
- Comment on your attitude and outstanding personality traits.

Usually three letters of reference are all you need. Many prospective employers send a reference check form to be filled out, or simply make a phone call.

Belloak Sportswriters
Academy
663 Belloak Drive
Belloak, Michigan 48666

Mr. Allen Calstrike
Editorial Director
I.C. Sportsview
Belloak County Line
6900 Bell River Drive
Belloak, Michigan 48666

Dear Mr Calstrike:

Kathy Kaken graduated from our academy in June this year with honors and a 3.65 grade point average. During the last year, I have worked closely with Kathy, assessing all facets of her total performance as a sportswriter.

She has many attributes that contribute to her excellence as a sportswriter, but the most impressive is her uncanny ability to interview reclusive athletes. She has unquestionably sound moral and ethical values that facilitate establishing instant rapport with others. Kathy's writing skills are superior, and she displays a well-placed, dry sense of humor. Well-liked by colleagues, subordinates, and superiors, Kathy contributes meaningfully to the team effort.

Kathy is punctual and reliable, conscientious and vivacious, showing a tremendous love for her profession. She exceeds requirements on all written assignments.

It is with great pleasure that I recommend Kathy, a superior student. She would be an asset to your newspaper's journalism department. If I may provide additional information, your inquiry is welcomed.

Respectfully,

W.W. Penwright, Ph.D.

Professor, Journalism

SECURE THE POSITION YOU WANT

Before you can secure the position you want, you must understand the employee selection process. Before the prospective employer ever reads your résumé and cover letter, he or she has a definite need to fill and has determined what qualifications and personality type will best meet that need. The purpose of the selection process is to determine which applicant makes a match.

. Phase 1 is to evaluate your résumé and cover letter. Phase 2 is the interview. Phase 3, your probationary period, is the final phase of the selection process.

Phase 1 of the selection process begins as the prospective employer glances at your envelope. Did you accurately type all the information? Did you include your return address? Is the contact person's name spelled correctly, and title included? Is the color of the envelope appropriate? As the prospective employer removes the contents from the envelope, does the paper match the envelope? Do all the pages match? Are they neatly or haphazardly folded? Let us stop for a moment. What could the reader surmise? Not much, you say? Wrong! The envelope can reveal whether you are neat, detail-oriented, accurate, and respectful to authority.

As the employer reads your cover letter, he or she can surmise from your list of accomplishments that you are energetic. Your grade point of 3.65 is remarkable. Your people skills indicate that you are probably a good communicator. Your letter is well organized, and your priorities have been established. You are progressive and results-oriented. You are courteous and self-confident with your self-addressed stamped envelope and your interview follow-up instructions, respectively. Within a minute, the employer has decided to read your résumé or to place you in the "no thanks" file. If your résumé portrays the same favorable traits, you may receive a letter or phone call with an invitation to an interview.

Your prospective employer will be prepared to ask you questions about your expertise, to assess your suitability for the position. By reviewing your Job-winning Package, you can deduce many of the likely questions. This should be the first step in your preinterview preparation.

Begin with a thorough mental, physical, psychological, and emotional assessment of your written package. What did you say in your cover letter and résumé? What questions might be asked about the contents of the enclosures? Remember, the employer's goal is to complete his or her sportswriting staff to achieve optimum coverage in all areas.

If your profession requires certification or state boards, one of the questions a prospective employer may ask is, "Will accepting a full-time position before taking your boards be too stressful?" Be prepared to state which of your qualities and skills will enable you to handle the stress, and your specific plans for coping with it. Information confirming the appointed date of your state boards would be helpful, and do not omit your permit. Refresh your memory, and if possible take pertinent documents with you to the interview. Will you

Retail sales personnel display sportswear for a potential customer.

need time off to study for and take the state boards? These arrangements should be agreed upon in advance. Be clear about your needs. If the company will not compromise to meet those needs before hiring, it could be a warning that your needs may be forgotten after employment.

You have emphasized your superior interpersonal skills. You may be asked hypothetical questions such as, "What would you do with this personality conflict?", which will reveal your attitude. Attitude is one of those intangibles that most people do not define but everyone recognizes. Attitude is a culmination of your personal self. You have taken a lifetime to learn and acquire your attitude. A good attitude is expected of health and fitness professionals, and often goes unrewarded; but a bad attitude is frequently the cause of problems and is quickly reprimanded. The importance of a good attitude is often underrated. Health and fitness professionals with excellent technical skills and superb educational qualifications have been released because of serious conflicts, when the underlying cause was really a bad attitude. Nothing compensates for a bad attitude. A negative, nothing-ever-goes-right, I-hate-to-work-here, know-it-all attitude is usually surrounded by needless problems. Most supervisors are adept at spotting a bad attitude a mile away. During an interview, a health and fitness candidate with a good attitude and lesser professional expertise (providing it is not substandard) will most likely be the one hired. The technically proficient health and fitness candidate with an unyielding attitude will be rejected. Skills and attitude are not synonymous, but a good attitude can go far in gaining you the guidance and support you need to nurture your technical skills. On the contrary, a bad attitude can be a direct ticket to the unemployment office.

As you prepare for your interview, keep in mind that your

future supervisor has many aspects to consider beyond the obvious. Budgetary allowance is a major consideration. Will you be the most cost-effective, as well as efficient, employee? Will your absenteeism rate be above average? Be ready to assure your prospective superior that your track record is good. Will you be the candidate to meet the newspaper's needs with the least additional training? Stress your outstanding accomplishments. Retention of personnel and length of service of employees are major factors in choosing employees. Emphasize your loyalty to the organization in exchange for its furthering your professional goals.

During the interview, your physical appearance and conduct will be evaluated. Pay particular attention to your grooming, attire, general health, and rest. Areas of conduct and behavior to receive special attention include: mental status, attitude, alertness, and knowledge of the subject being discussed. The emotional state to project is one of calm, appropriate responses and self-confidence. The psychological state of mind should display active communication, particularly nonverbal, and socially acceptable coping mechanisms. A very important factor to your success is to know yourself. You can then answer any questions asked about your interactions, reactions and actions, your stress level, others' perception of you, and your perception of others. No one can advise you how to respond to specific questions, but knowing yourself and responding honestly is your best assurance of finding the ideal position.

Interviews need not be painful if you are prepared. Thanks to your presearch, you know your destination, the best route to take, travel time, and how to find the director's office.

Your personal presentment should reflect the position you are seeking. You should always dress in tastefully conservative business attire. Men should wear a suit. For women, a skirt and blazer or a dress with matching jacket is appropriate. Pants suits are not acceptable. A chief executive officer mistakenly sent an applicant to maid services because she was dressed in blue jeans. Gentlemen, save the female-catching aftershave for another day. Pay special attention to your grooming. Ladies, no jewelry or makeup that screams "Look at me!"

From the second you walk into the building, be acutely aware of your personal presentment. Go to the rest room and make one last head-to-toe inspection of your appearance. At the door of the interviewer's office, remember that every move or comment you make can count. Think about your posture, handshake, eye contact, gestures, and nervous habits. You can bet your future that the interviewer will.

As you wait, quietly read a career-oriented or neutral magazine. When invited into the office, offer a handshake, introduce yourself, and wait for an invitation to be seated. The tone of the interview can be set by those three things. Was the introduction formal or informal? Was the seating arrangement openly friendly and approachable, or aloof and authoritarian? Was the handshake assertive, passive, or aggressive?

The format of a typical interview is a straightforward question and answer exchange. Chances are that it will open with confirmation of the information presented in your cover letter and résumé. Before it closes you will probably be given an opportunity to ask questions that have not been answered. If not, by all means ask! You can effectively close the interview by asking whether you are a viable candidate. Be prepared for a rejection if you choose this closing, but usually it is the transition into your interview follow-up discussion. A tour of the company gives you yet another opportunity to let your five senses work for you, and can be an indication that you are indeed a viable candidate.

As a rule, personnel people are a close-knit group of professionals. If the interviewer thinks the information you have given may be inaccurate, or that you sound too good to be true, he or she will probably check with a few colleagues. There is no easy escape if you have earned a poor reputation. If you have major problems, your only chance for survival is to admit them and work to change each one. If you are not at fault for an incident, honestly explain your point of view.

An interviewer's questions are specifically relevant to the position you seek. Most states have guidelines on questions an employer can and cannot legally ask. Write to the Department of Civil Rights in your state for a copy of *Pre-Employment Inquiry Guide*. The following are typical questions:

Detail your major accomplishments. How did you talk Mr. Slokno into an interview when other well-known sportswriters were refused?

How soon do you hope to progress to a managerial position? What managerial experience do you think you will need? Can you analyze problems effectively, and are you capable of initiating a solution? Give me an example. (Your communication skills will be silently assessed.)

Would you react if an athlete verbally abused you?

Why have you chosen our small-town newspaper as a place of employment? (If you presearched your prospective employer, you will be able to answer intelligently.) Precisely what can you do for this company? (Insert your skills, and state your career goals upon hiring.) Will you be able to handle the position? Do you possess the skills, knowledge, and experience to carry the job? If hired, will you be punctual? Will you put in a productive day's work?

How long will you stay satisfactorily employed at this company? How long do you estimate it will take you to master the job and become profitable to the organization?

Will you work well with your colleagues and the interviewer? Are you a self-starter, or do you need to be cranked?

As you answer the questions, the interviewer will compare your responses to those of other applicants and draw conclusions during the interview.

As you terminate the interview, keep in mind that if you are not hired, there may be good reasons. It could be to your advantage. Company executives are expert at putting a team together, and your personality may not be compatible. Or your professional growth could be stifled, or the newspaper's philosophies are in direct conflict with yours. Your skills may be substandard for this particular newspaper's requirements; consider the consequences to your professional and personal integrity if your skills were not comparable to staff of the same classification. Before you feel rejected, or that the interview was a waste, look objectively at all the facts.

Whether the interview was negative or positive, thank your prospective employer before you leave. Once outside, make notes on your Prospective Employer Card and prepare to write your postinterview follow-up.

At home, write a thank-you note for the interview. The note should state its purpose and the major issues and points discussed during the interview. You should confirm your understanding of the prospective employer's comments. Thank the receptionist and others you met for their hospitality, and say a kind word or two about the company. Finally, add to or correct impressions left behind.

Kathy Kaken
2020 Wishing Well Drive
Quindle, Michigan 48509
1-111-888-2525

Mr. Allen Calstrike
Editorial Director
I.C. Sportsview
Belloak County Line
6900 Bell River Drive
Belloak, Michigan 48666

Dear Mr. Calstrike:

I am interested in the position as a sportswriter that I interviewed for on July 1 and would truly appreciate your consideration.

I enclose my supplemental and corresponding transcripts for you to review at your convenience. As you recommended, I contacted Mr. Steuber. I am scheduled to meet with him on July 6 to demonstrate interview techniques to sportswriters in Division A.

A special thank-you to Kay Evans, your receptionist, for her kind assistance and for offering refreshments. Your time, explanations, and consideration are greatly appreciated. I look forward to working with you in the near future.

Respectfully,

Kathy Kaken

STRUCTURE THE POSITION YOU WANT

How will you handle your probationary or orientation period? When you are hired, you are usually given an orientation period to familiarize yourself with the company, and you are sometimes considered on probation for a period of time. Individual company policy dictates the time, but it is commonly three months. During this period, your immediate supervisor observes and evaluates you on the job. All aspects of your performance, from your technical skills to your attitude, are taken into consideration before it is decided whether you will be retained as a permanent employee. This is the last major checkpoint before the launch into permanent ties. While your employer is evaluating you, you should be examining your employer. Take advantage of your golden time of assessment.

- Learn the systems of the facility.
- Ask any questions that occur to you.
- Establish and perfect your daily routines.
- Present your facts to your superior. Make a special effort to address any problems you may encounter. This is the time to solve them, or at least confront them honestly.
- Assess your skills in relation to your position and to colleagues performing identical functions.
- Implement steps to improve your weak points.
- Make plans for your advancement at this employer.
- Form your communication network of superiors, colleagues, and subordinates.
- Weigh the benefits against the disadvantages of the position.
- Make a smooth transition to permanent employment, or professionally make your departure.

Just as an employer has the right to release you without obligation during the probationary period, you have the right to resign without using the employer as a reference. If you have decided this is not what you want, resign amicably.

You have been employed for six months, the afternoon editorial director position will be vacant in two months, and you want a promotion. Critically evaluate your status to determine if you are qualified for and really want the position. If possible, talk with the present editorial director to find out what hidden responsibilities the job may have. Strip the glory, and then decide if you want the extra hours and headaches that come with the job. What financial reward will you receive for the advancement? What changes do you foresee in schedule, team members, superiors, and environment? Will you be responsible for any new machines? Will you be in a new location?

Check out all the details. If they please you, follow your employer's promotion procedures to the last detail. Complete and submit forms to the proper person. When you apply for the promotion, dress and act accordingly. Pay special attention to your grooming, etiquette, and conduct. Be careful not to be too social. Business is business, and familiarity can backfire.

Let's say you were denied the promotion, and you feel you would be better appreciated elsewhere. If you quit, leave the door open behind you. You never know when that open door may be a welcome sight under new circumstances. Even if the conditions do not meet your standards, do not leave angry; just leave. Your termination should remain friendly and in accord with good business ethics.

Know when it is time for you to move on. Has your professional expertise been stifled or stunted? Are you a victim of burnout? Shame on you! Get in touch with yourself! As you prepare to resign, write a letter of resignation to your immediate supervisor, briefly explaining why you are leaving and when. Above all, express thanks for the opportunity of having been an employee. Submit the letter as soon as feasible. That allows preparations to be made to replace you, while maintaining cohesion of the unit and facilitating a smooth transition.

Kathy Kaken
2020 Wishing Well Drive
Quindle, Michigan 48509

Mr. Allen Calstrike
Editorial Director
I. C. Sportsview
Belloak County Line
6900 Bell River Drive
Belloak, Michigan 48666

Dear Mr. Calstrike:

I regretfully submit my resignation on this date, June 15, 1990, effective June 29, 1990.

I plan to pursue a bachelor of science degree in sports journalism at Belloak University on a full-time basis.

During my tenure, I have gained much knowledge in the high-tech world of sports editing and management. I wish to thank you for your assistance toward attaining my ultimate goals.

The employees I have worked with are terrific, and I will miss everyone. Good luck in your future endeavors.

Respectfully,

Kathy Kaken

Request an exit interview with your immediate supervisor, the Human Resources Department, or any authority to whom you can give an honest appraisal. You will want to review your personnel file, to discuss why you are leaving as honestly as possible, and to offer suggestions for changes that would create a more positive work atmosphere. Some badly needed changes may not be mentioned by employees for fear of job loss. You are free to say what you want within reason. Use this opportunity to say goodbye and express your appreciation. This is the time to request references.

An exit interview differs sharply from an entrance interview. Its purpose is to close any communication gaps and terminate a business relationship. Conduct during an exit interview can be informal and led by either you or the employer.

Before you walk out the door for the last time as an employee, complete all ongoing projects. Tie the loose ends so that the next sportswriter can pick up where you left off. Offer to orient your replacement. Give the next sportswriter the added edge that will make the job easier. Help everyone to achieve a smooth transition. Put in a full day's work on your last day. You owe it to yourself, for everyone's memories of you to be pleasant.

Before closing Chapter IV a trio of sensitive issues and an exciting venture need to be addressed.

Legal, Moral, and Ethical Obligations

Legal obligations are the laws that bind you. Rules, regulations, laws, and procedures all refer to the boundaries within which you must contain your business transactions. Who establishes the laws that govern your career choice? All careers are controlled to some degree by federal, state, and

What would you consider the aerobics instructor's legal, moral, and ethical obligations?

local laws written to standardize and regulate all types of business transactions for the purpose of promoting the public well-being. Medically oriented professions are particularly subject to state or federal laws designed to standardize and regulate their activities. Every career is governed by employer-dictated policies, procedures, and by-laws. Specialty organizations have well-established and often elaborate by-laws, rules, and regulations.

Failure to abide by any law can result in legal prosecution. Our judicial system is inflexible and unforgiving of excuses for breaking the laws. Ignorance of a law does not grant immunity from prosecution. To avoid vulnerability, learn the laws that regulate your career.

Moral issues are less definitive than legal issues and may not be documented for you to rehearse and perfect. However, you have had many years of practice struggling with moral issues. For our purposes, moral refers to right, "socially acceptable," and wrong, "unacceptable, antisocial" behavior.

Consider the following illustration. You are employed by a large corporation. You inadvertently drop a pen into your pocket or purse. Once home, you realize that you have a company pen. You shrug, drop the pen into the junk drawer, and dismiss the matter with, "Oh well, the company has more money than I do. They won't miss one little pen. Besides, they don't pay me what I'm worth anyway." A trivial incident? Maybe. Qualify the word "maybe." Stealing is stealing, and it was only borrowed? First you borrow, then you return. If an item is not returned or paid for, then it is not borrowed, is it?

The way you handle moral issues is an individual matter. Poor judgment regarding a supposedly trivial moral issue can cause irreparable damage to your personal integrity and professional image. Be aware of and accountable for your own actions.

Ethical issues are more complex, yet subtle. What is really fair, or right, or equal for a given group of people regarding a specific problem? Sometimes that question cannot be answered to please every person involved. Take a minute or two to think of an ethical problem you have solved recently.

Being an Entrepreneur

Entrepreneurs are the future. A career in health and fitness can often be converted to an entrepreneur's paradise. However, there are a multitude of overt and covert complexities to owning your own business. To be a successful entrepreneur, you must carefully balance the scale of *professional expertise* acquired through training and experience, and *business skills*. Be patient with yourself before you begin a business. Learn to evaluate yourself and the business. Be sure your career and personal goals are compatible. If incompatibilities are apparent, make adaptations *before* you open a business. If you are unable to restructure your career and personal goals to achieve a harmonious balance, resolve the discrepancies before proceeding.

Evaluate your entrepreneurial personality type by these criteria:

- Are you imaginative, resourceful, and self-disciplined?
- Do you detest regimentation and can you take calculated risks (financial and otherwise)?
- Are you assertive?
- Are you an effective communicator?
- Can you function independently, while motivating other key personnel?
- Are you able to initiate change?

Evaluate the business by these criteria:

- What do you expect the business to do for you?
- What needs of yours will it meet, bypass, ignore, challenge, or insult?
- What special abilities or capabilities do you bring to the business to give it a distinctive style?
- What motivates, interests, and intrigues you about this business?

Are your technical expertise and business skills adequate to meet market needs and give you the competitive edge?

- Gain a solid educational and professional foundation. That is time and effort you will be glad you spent.
- Take a few business courses to learn the basics of entrepreneurship.
- Take time to learn each facet of the business in its entirety before leaping to the next. Do not scatter your efforts. Master one entity at a time, remembering that time is money and without money you have no business. The best way to learn how to be a thriving entrepreneur is to first work for one.

Work for the type of company you want to own long enough to grasp the intricacies of daily activity, both the common and uncommon. For instance, if you want to own and operate your own health spa, you need to know all the aspects of health and fitness training, the by-laws (if purchasing an established business), the laws governing the business (state, local, federal), and the regulatory rules and regulations under which you must function.

"Little things" that keep the business running smoothly

must be taken care of at regular intervals. Who is responsible for set-up and maintenance of the equipment? How often must the equipment be checked? Who is qualified to test the equipment's functionality? Who is responsible for hiring personnel, handling worker's compensation or negligence claims? Does the company retain an attorney? Who is responsible for orientation of new employees? Must you hire a public relations consultant to do the marketing and advertising, or are you qualified? Do you know the details of profit margin, rate setting, and paying taxes, or should you retain a CPA? What does your competition offer their clients?

Research all aspects of a business enterprise before you begin to set up a business. Advice on entrepreneurship abounds in books, pamphlets, and through government and private organizations. One of many books available is: *How to Pick the Right Small Business Opportunity*, by K. J. Albert; McGraw-Hill, $6.95 paperback.

Remember, if the business sounds utterly perfect, put your checkbook back in your pocket until you have checked it out with the Better Business Bureau, the state regulatory agency, or the specialty organization. Reach for the Milky Way, but keep both feet on earth.

Chapter V

The Health and Fitness Zone of the 1990s

Have you read the "best of life"–type section of your local paper, scanned the classified advertisements, or viewed a television health-related program or the special "living right" segment of the news broadcast recently? If you have not, do so this evening. You will be fascinated by the new and exciting happenings in the health and fitness area. You will discover the expanding role of health and fitness professionals in conventional job prospects and be introduced to unusual employment opportunities as they emerge. Here are a few career options that job forecasters expect to be in demand in the 1990s.

Unique challenges for health and fitness professionals abound in the 1990s. Public relations, marketing, and sales positions are flourishing in several areas. New and expanding health and fitness–oriented services and products employ public relations, marketing, and sales people. The possibilities are almost limitless. Everything from health foods to exercise equipment, to health spas, to weight loss clinics seek the expertise of a health and fitness professional to promote their business. If you are capable of increasing sales and generating a substantial profit, you will be amply rewarded with your base salary plus commission. (Commissions or profit-sharing can exceed the base salary for some people.) Some companies pay travel expenses and provide a company car in addition to the conventional benefits package. Salaries range from $16,000 to over $100,000 per year;

however, do not be fooled by the top figure. As usual, there can be a dark side to these high-energy public relations–type positions. Have you guessed it? Several variables that you have no control over will affect your profit margin. Is your product or service seasonal? Will economic hard times adversely affect your position? Do you like to travel, locally or over your territory? Do you enjoy after-hours business functions? If the dark side does not darken your interest, you may have discovered the ideal employment prospect.

While you are still prospecting, consider nutrition. Health and fitness careers in this discipline are growing at a phenomenal rate. Consumers have become more cognizant of healthful food and eating habits. Restaurants, grocery stores, health clubs, hospitals, newspapers, and television networks are all employing health and fitness professionals to gather and present information to and for the consumer.

Nutritionists and registered dietitians may function as consultants, teachers, researchers, quality-assurance specialists, or other roles compatible with professional qualifications and client needs. Financial compensation for dietitians/nutritionists can be outstanding with the right credentials and for the right clients. Choose your training program and employer wisely. The need for dietitians/nutritionists is expected to continue to grow during the next decade.

Perhaps you would enjoy more physical activity. What about becoming a physical education teacher, health club instructor, coach, or athletic trainer? Consider two of its greatest attributes: stability and helping others achieve their goals. As long as people of all ages remain enthusiastic about health and fitness, the need for specialty instructors will remain high. The medical community has endorsed and promoted the virtues of exercise. During the past year, comprehensive evaluations and studies have been conducted by research specialists to prove the value of exercise for all age groups. Two studies of primary interest could offer many job prospects worth pursuing, or at least researching.

- The first specialty for health and fitness trainers/instructors is children. Children, their parents, teachers, physicians, and significant other caregivers are taking preventive measures to delay, reduce, or prevent middle-aged health concerns. This new awareness and active response to anticipated needs is creating many career options specifically designed to meet the young child's needs.
- The age group targeted in the other study is older adults. Here are some interesting facts to consider. Older adults are more active and health-conscious and constitute a larger proportion of the population than in the past. The percentage is expected to increase during the next decade. One of the major concerns of medical professionals is exercise/activity individualized to meet each client's physical, emotional, social, psychological, and intellectual needs and expectations. The challenge is great, and so are the financial rewards for the health and fitness professional who responds appropriately to client needs. Salaries are $30,000 plus, depending on whether corporate, private, or public client/employer.

Why not consider being a research specialist to discover the best way to exercise safely and effectively or answer a host of other health and fitness inquiries asked by professionals. Research specialists have first access to privileged information even before medical professionals. Often they are the ones who uncover the information or recognize the need for more data in a given area. Research specialists are needed in many branches of the health and fitness industry. Check your newspaper's classified ad section, a local university, or large hospital for some of the positions available. Ask product and service managers about their greatest needs. Many will cite research specialists to perfect their health and fitness–related product or service, develop a new or better product or service, or research consumer needs in a given health or fitness area. Salaries are $30,000 and above, depending on the usual variables of qualifications, geographic location, and employer whether public, private, corporate, or government agency.

The demand for physical therapists far exceeds the current supply throughout the United States. Employment opportunities abound in a variety of settings ranging from sports team, to hospital, to consultant who travels from one site to another. Responsibilities can encompass many levels of involvement from program development and implementation to one-on-one client/therapist rapport. Financial compensation often starts between $30,000 and $40,000.

Why not look at the possibility of being a health and fitness motivator. A "motivating manager," CEO (chief executive officer), or athletic administrator, regardless of exact title and company, is always in demand. Any company, large or small, that employs staff to perform tasks needs a qualified health and fitness manager. The motivating manager who can provide a superior quality of product or service, substantially reduce costs, increase profits, and motivate the employees to perform at their optimum will certainly be hired. Remember that the number of management positions is proportionately less than health and fitness line positions for that service or product. Managers are frequently seasoned veterans. However, you could be the exception to the rule. Managers' salaries vary from $16,000 in a small retail health and fitness shop to over $100,000 for athletic director.

One of the first entities we discussed was sales, public

relations, and marketing in health and fitness. Let us be a little more specific about career opportunities in one aspect of health and fitness—retail outlets. Everyone who manufactures a product or offers a service must convince health and fitness–conscious consumers that their wares are the best available for the fee they charge. Hence, the need for qualified sales, public relations, and marketing people. The competition for the consumers' money is fierce. For instance, the next time you visit a sporting goods store, notice the number of companies that manufacture running shoes and the many designs offered in each company's line. That is only one example. Again, the base salary may not bulge your wallet, but commissions and profit-sharing help.

These are only a few of the bright job prospects in the health and fitness field. Most of the careers discussed in the book hold a promising future. Statistician is the only one in imminent danger of extinction.

To complement the bright job forecasts, salaries are expected to rise commensurate with the profitability of the products or services. As always, your qualifications, educational preparation, and personal ability to thrive in the work world all contribute to your salary.

with the clientele. Leaving my well-established extended family to start all over again is not a decision to take lightly.

Casondra Simmons

My career success story is still being created. I am a sophomore attending a four-year university. I drifted in limbo for three terms until I studied this career exploration process, and this is what I decided to do!

I know I want to pursue a career as a research specialist, an exercise physiologist (medical or educational), or in biomechanics (medical or educational). I haven't reached a final decision, but educational exercise physiologist is very appealing. The basic requirements for all three are similar; that's the beauty. One will be my favorite, and the others will be my alternate career choices.

The university I am attending is fully accredited to teach all my career choices. I am here on a scholarship through the university's financial assistance program, and I supplement my income by working part time at a sports medicine research center, which gives me exposure to the kind of work I want. I plan to seek full-time employment at the center. When I discussed the prospect with the chief executive officer, I was assured that such positions are not readily filled and that a vacancy could be created to accommodate a qualified research specialist.

I am very comfortable and confident in the high-tech, fast-paced, intriguing world of sports research. Any aspect of my life that I've had to restructure to accommodate my career, I have done unconsciously. I am so absorbed in my work and happy with my life-style that I'm not interested in making changes.

Index